D1282506

The
Williams–Siegel
Documentary

BY ELI SIEGEL

Hot Afternoons Have Been in Montana: Poems

Hail, American Development

*James and the Children: A Consideration of
Henry James's* The Turn of the Screw

The Aesthetic Method in Self-Conflict

Psychiatry, Economics, Aesthetics

Is Beauty the Making One of Opposites?

*The Modern Quarterly Beginnings of
Aesthetic Realism: 1922–1923*

THE
WILLIAMS–SIEGEL
DOCUMENTARY

Including

Williams' Poetry Talked about
by Eli Siegel,
and William Carlos Williams
Present and Talking: 1952

EDITED BY MARTHA BAIRD AND ELLEN REISS

DEFINITION PRESS   NEW YORK

Library of Congress Catalog Card Number 70-100610

Standard Book Number 910492-12-3

Manufactured in the United States of America
by the Haddon Craftsmen.

Acknowledgments

Our thanks for permission to use extensive quotations from the
following:

"Vistas," from *The Selected Poems of Alfred Kreymborg
1912–1944,* Copyright, 1945, by Alfred Kreymborg. Reprinted
by permission of E. P. Dutton & Co.

Lines from "The Hollow Men" in *Collected Poems 1909–1962*
by T. S. Eliot, copyright, 1936, by Harcourt, Brace & World,
Inc.: copyright, © 1963, 1964 by T. S. Eliot. Reprinted by permission of the publisher.

Passages from *Kora in Hell,* Copyright © 1957 by William
Carlos Williams. Reprinted by permission of City Lights Books.

Prefatory Information

The first form of this work, published by the Terrain Gallery in 1964, contained Williams' 1951 letter and excerpts from Siegel's 1952 lecture on Williams' poetry with the discussion between Siegel and Williams following. The entire lecture is now presented, as transcribed from the original recording, slightly edited for publication. The talk was given extemporaneously, as Eli Siegel's lectures always are.

For the present work we have gathered other documents to present the Williams-Siegel story: how Williams' letter came to be written, how Siegel's lecture came to be given, what happened and what didn't happen.

A good many facts are negative. They consist of absences and silences. There is no way of documenting these except by mentioning them. For example, Williams mentioned the editor of the Golden Goose Press only once. Of the persons he suggested be invited to hear Siegel's talk, only Harold Norse came. The persons Siegel invited all declined. Lloyd Frankenberg and Louis Untermeyer did not attend the Museum of Modern Art reading. Mrs. Williams met the Siegels once only, briefly, at the Museum of Modern Art.

Because we were denied permission to quote any of William Carlos Williams' poems in their entirety, we have quoted a few lines according to the critical necessities of this book and in keeping with the "fair use"

v

provision of the copyright law, indicating in a footnote exactly what was originally quoted and where it can be found in current editions of Williams works.

That this is an inconvenience to the reader, we are regretfully aware; but the reason for it is part of the Williams-Siegel story, which it is the purpose of this book to tell as exactly, fairly, and completely as possible.

Williams himself gave written permission for the publication of his letter to Martha Baird of November 3, 1951. The content of his other letters was summarized in the journal entries of Martha Baird, which are included.

When the events recorded here began, in 1951, Williams at sixty-eight was on the first crest of his large fame, which followed the publication of *Paterson* in 1948.

In 1951, Eli Siegel was forty-nine and had been teaching Aesthetic Realism for ten years. He and his wife, Martha Baird, lived and worked on Jane Street, New York City, where he gave lectures, classes, and Aesthetic Realism lessons.

Aesthetic Realism arose out of poetry and the teaching of poetry; it is a new kind of education which includes, for the first time, the aesthetic criticism of self. "The world, art, and self explain each other," Siegel says; "each is the aesthetic oneness of opposites."

The beginning of this idea is in Siegel's *Nation* Prize poem of 1925, "Hot Afternoons Have Been in Montana," which affected Williams so profoundly. These lines from "Hot Afternoons" were quoted in the preface to the first Aesthetic Realism publication, *The Aesthetic Method in Self-Conflict* of 1946:

There are millions of men in the world, and each is
    one man;
Each is one man by himself, taking care of himself
    all the time, and changing other men and being
    changed by them;
The quiet of this afternoon is strange, haunting,
    awful. . . .

Contents

1 THE WILLIAMS LETTER AND OTHER
   DOCUMENTS   1
   October 1951–March 1952

   Williams' letter to Martha Baird about Siegel's
   poems—"He has outstripped the world of his
   time." Siegel's letter to Williams. Martha
   Baird's journal describes Williams' visit to the
   Siegels; he invites Siegel to read at Museum of
   Modern Art; talk of poetry; D. H. Lawrence
   and Baudelaire; Williams' feeling about his
   letter; his feeling when writing a poem; Siegel
   to talk on Williams' poems. More letters.
   Siegel speaks to his class about Williams.
   Date for Siegel's talk confirmed.

2 WILLIAMS' POETRY TALKED ABOUT BY
   ELI SIEGEL, AND WILLIAM CARLOS
   WILLIAMS PRESENT AND TALKING   33
   March 5, 1952

   "Convivio." Eliot and Williams distinguished.
   Siegel's 1934 *Scribner's* review of WCW.
   René Taupin on Williams. *Paterson.* Pound
   on Williams. Quantum theory in relation to
   the poetic line. *Others,* 1916. Williams compared to Kreymborg, Pound, Eliot. "Tract."
   Musical passages in the short stories. "Pasto-

ral." Animadversions on some poets. "Young Sycamore." "Portrait of the Author." Rest and motion in Williams, in the poetic line, and in the world. "Spring and All." Williams and Coleridge. Williams and one more way of seeing the world. *Kora in Hell* underestimated by its author. Leigh Hunt and George Saintsbury. Comparison of *Kora in Hell* to *Paterson.* "The Red Wheelbarrow" and Tennyson. "Rapid Transit." "The Cure."

Discussion following lecture   93

Williams says: "It's as if everything I've ever done has been for you." He talks of his letter about Siegel again. "Hamlet Revisited." The sonnet. A mistake about Chaucer and Dryden. Immortality and Shakespeare. *Kora in Hell* again. WCW says, "You've opened up a lot of new territory for me"; describes writing "Portrait of the Author." Will come when Siegel talks on *Hamlet.*

3 LETTERS AND JOURNALS   107
   March 1952–December 1957

1952—Further comments from Martha Baird's journal on Siegel's talk; WCW says he hasn't written a poem in years, and has been encouraged. Description of Museum of Modern Art reading. Williams does not come to Siegel's talk on *Hamlet.* Siegel's phone call to Williams. Two letters. 1954—Williams refuses *The Folio* permission to print his letter about Siegel. Martha Baird's letter to Williams. His reply gives permission for use of the letter. 1957—*Hot Afternoons Have Been in Montana: Poems* published with Williams' letter.   Nominated for National Book Award. Williams' introduction to new edition of *Kora in Hell;* his silence about Siegel.

4   SUPPLEMENTARY DOCUMENTS
     BY ELI SIEGEL   139
     1955–1967

     T. S. Eliot and W. C. Williams: A Distinction   141
     (*The University of Kansas City Review,* 1955)

     Letter to Thomas De Baggio   147
     (*Washington Independent,* 1967)

     Review of *The William Carlos Williams Reader*   152
     (*Washington Independent,* 1967)

     First Thoughts on the Williams Holding
     Company   168
     (*Washington Independent,* 1967)

5   AFTERWORD BY ELLEN REISS   173

Comparison of WCW letter about Siegel to statements about other poets—Ginsberg, Stevens, Sandburg, Auden, Frost.   Relation of Williams' conflict to experiences of the writer. March 1952 letter of WCW to Robert Lowell. "Asphodel, That Greeny Flower."   Arnold, Coleridge, Siegel as critics.

APPENDIX   197

Definition Press, New Directions, and Permissions: A Short History

INDEX   201

1

The Williams Letter
and Other Documents
October 1951–March 1952

Part One

EDITORS' NOTE. *In October 1951, Sheldon Kranz, a student of Aesthetic Realism with Eli Siegel, was teaching at Long Island University and doing book reviews for the* Brooklyn Eagle. *He had reviewed William Carlos Williams'* Autobiography, *which gave him the idea of writing to Williams about Siegel's poetry. Sheldon Kranz's letter, of which we have no copy, mentioned two groups of poems the Society for Aesthetic Realism had mimeographed which he would like Williams to see.*

On October 21, Williams sent a postcard in reply, saying Siegel had always been regarded as a one-poem poet, but send the poems and include return postage.

MARTHA BAIRD TO W. C. WILLIAMS

Society for Aesthetic Realism
New York, October 26, 1951

Dear Dr. Williams:

I have heard from Sheldon Kranz of his correspondence with you and am happy to send you, on behalf of the Society, two groups of poems by Eli

Siegel. We want the author of "The Red Wheelbarrow" to have them as a gift.

I was much affected by your readiness to "call attention to good work which has been neglected." One might expect this to be the response of any just person, but one sees it so seldom. It is good to see it now.

We feel the poems we are sending you are beautiful, and if you find them so too, it will mean a lot. If you care for the poems, you may be interested to see a list of publications of the Society, which contains writings by Mr. Siegel in other fields, some of them surprising.

Sincerely yours,
MARTHA BAIRD, *Secretary*

The poems—sixty-one in all—included the 1925 Nation *Prize poem (the source of the "one poem" reputation) and a number of others which had appeared in journals such as* Blues, Hound & Horn, Modern Quarterly, *mostly during the 1920s and early 30s. The poems in the first group, on which Williams' reply is based, were:*

Hot Afternoons Have Been in Montana
Ralph Isham, 1753 and Later
Somewhere This
Duke of Parma's Ear
Worms Go South and They Fit In

Macaw: Lions
In Dark Discovered
Certain Things
Smoke Goes Up Slowly
She's Crazy and It Means Something
One Question ("I—/Why?")
Familiar Mad Heroine
Quiet, Tears, Babies
Gone Rain
It Will Be Annabel November
Miss Edith Lindsay and Form
Partly
She, So Longed For
Love and Jobs
Must I Wait All My Life; or, The Misery Song
The Missouri
Lines on Eternity
Encomium of Desire
*Let Fat Men, in Plush Coats, Do as They Please
    a Little*
Lamps Also for This
The Grasses All Loving
Alfred-Seeable Philadelphia Sky
Meadow and a Stem
Night in 1242
Hell, What Is This About, Asked Again
A Hundred Plants on an Estate

Most of these are now in Hot Afternoons Have
Been in Montana: Poems *(New York: Definition
Press, 1957).*

W. C. WILLIAMS TO MARTHA BAIRD

Rutherford, New Jersey
November 3, 1951

My dear Martha Baird:

I cannot adequately thank you for first writing me and then sending me the copies of Eli Siegel's poems. I am thrilled: your communications could not have come at a better time. I can't tell you how important Siegel's work is in the light of my present understanding of the modern poem. He belongs in the very first rank of our living artists. That he has not been placed there by our critics (what good are they?) is the inevitable result of their colonialism, their failure to understand the significance, the compulsions, broadened base upon which prosody rests in the modern world and our opportunity and obligations when we concern ourselves with it.

We are not up to Siegel, even yet. The basic criteria have not been laid bare. It's a long hard road to travel with only starvation fare for us on the way. Almost everyone wants to run back to the old practices. You can't blame him. He wants assurance, security, the approval that comes to him from established practices. He wants to be united with his fellows. He wants the "beautiful," that is to say . . . the past. It is a very simple and very powerful urge. It puts the hardest burdens on the pioneer who while recognizing the virtues and glories of the past sees its restricting and malevolent fixations. Siegel knows this in his own person. He must be tough and supremely gifted.

The thing that particularly interests me, after a lifetime of pondering the matter, is the technical implication. To me it's black and white: either a man has quit or gone forward. And if he's gone forward he's headed straight into disrepute. People aren't up to it. And of those who are for you almost no one knows why. It's all right to speak of aesthetic realism and you've done good work to get behind a man such as Siegel. But it goes deeper than that—or until I understand you better I have to assume it. But Siegel isn't for me an aesthete or not primarily an aesthete; he's an intensely practical professional writer who has outstripped the world of his time in several very important respects. Technical respects.

I have to presume that he knows absolutely what he is doing and why he is doing it. I think he does. That doesn't explain, quite, how he happened to hit on the just qualities of his style in the first place— a lot of talk and verification would have to be spilled over that before we'd know each other there. But he did hit a major chord and from the first, with his major poem "Hot Afternoons" etc. Only today do I realize how important that poem is in the history of our development as a cultural entity—a place which is continually threatened and which we may never attain unless we develop the position which HE has secured for us. I say definitely that that single poem, out of a thousand others written in the past quarter century, secures our place in the cultural world.

I make such a statement only after a lifetime of thought and experience, I make it deliberately. How Siegel got himself, undamaged by the past, to that position is a puzzle to me. But all genius presents unsolvable puzzles as to their origin. In any case he did, unspoiled; got to an absolutely unspoiled point of practice which no one (not even himself perhaps) was able adequately to grasp. On that rock and only on that rock can we in our cultural pattern build. And being the darlings of our era, the ones who must break with the past (as Toynbee recognizes—tho some of us saw it before him) we are obliged to follow what Siegel instinctively set down. We are compelled to pursue his lead. Everything we most are compelled to do is in that one poem.

The immediate effect is of surprise, as with everything truly new, technical surprise. There is nothing, not even an odor of Elizabethan English (on which *all* our training is founded. How he escaped THAT is beyond me.). As I read his pieces I am never prepared for what will come next, either the timing or the imagery. I simply do not know what he's going to say next or how he's going to say it.

This is powerful evidence of a new track. The mind that made that mark is a different mind from ours. It is following different incentives. The eyes back of it are new eyes. They are seeing something different from ours. The evidence is technical but it comes out at the non-technical level as either great pleasure to the beholder, a deeper taking of the breath, a feeling of cleanliness, which is the sign of the truly new. The other side of the picture is the extreme resentment that a fixed sclerotic mind feels confronting this new. It shows itself by the violent opposition Siegel received from the "authorities" whom I shall not dignify by naming and after that by neglect, an inevitable neglect due not to resentment but by the sheer inability of the general mind to grasp what has taken place.

Even a person such as myself, who has been searching for a solid footing, feeling about in the mud of the times for it while the rain and the hail of opinion batters about my head—even I was not up to a full or any realization of what the *Narr*, the "fool," Siegel had done. But at last I am just beginning to know, to know firmly what the present day mind is seeking. I finally have caught a glimmer of the basic place which we, today, must occupy. And I have realized our place, in this cultural field, which is inevitably to be ours, to fill or to fail. We're only hanging on by our teeth and fingernails now, or even, today, loosing our grip. I think today we are (temporarily, I hope) slipping back.

For those who are working in the materials, the despised technicians, it's a heartbreaking as it is a difficult and often exasperating battle. That's why I say it's thrilling to have had you redirect my attention to Siegel.

What I can do to be of practical assistance to you in pushing Siegel's work, so monumentally neglected, I don't know. It is incredible that he has not been published. And it is just like a man like that, it seems always to come out that way (he is satisfied with the *inner* warmth and does not need external assurances) not to care, not to have pushed himself forward. Instinctively he knows what his significance is. He can afford to wait. But it is time now to bring him forward and I don't quite know what to do.

I can give a reading of his works and I'd be glad to do so at some favorable opportunity; I can't give much time for I am harassed by the importunities of my life as is everyone else. I have to write whenever I am able and when I turn away from that for even the most laudable purposes I feel as if I were losing my life's very blood, irreparably. There is so much to do and there is so little time.

You say Siegel is alive and working. Greet him for me and tell him of this letter. I congratulate you on the intelligent direction of your work and the heart behind it.

> Sincerely yours,
> WILLIAM CARLOS WILLIAMS

MARTHA BAIRD TO W. C. WILLIAMS

> New York
> November 13, 1951

Dear William Carlos Williams:

Your letter was very beautiful. It was overwhelming. I think it will do much good. I hope the writing of it has made you happier. The letter will help our Society and it has startled delightfully my husband (for Eli Siegel is my husband).

We are still in a surprised field. It is so hard to answer such a letter. The word for it is noble. I think it stands for the truth.

Let this do for a while. I shall write to you again, or Eli shall, when we are less astonished.

Our most beautiful wishes to you.

> Sincerely,
> MARTHA BAIRD

ELI SIEGEL TO W. C. WILLIAMS

New York
December 5, 1951

Dear William Carlos Williams:

It has taken me all this while to see your letter in some perspective, and I hope you haven't felt it was incorrect to take so long answering one of the most beautiful and courageous documents I have ever seen.

When you write about poetry in America, I am moved immensely. I cannot say you are wrong at all, when you say I have been seen unjustly in the past. It is so. And Poetry and America have meant so much to me, it is very hard to say how much, in a personal way.

How should poetry be written? That is the question all through your letter. I have felt in the last twenty years or so, that you were in the midst of poetry. I said so, in *Scribner's* in 1934. I have said so since. In a talk on "Poetry and Technique," I talked of you as on poetry's side.

Yet how surprised I was by your communication. I had a memory of something so different from kindness about Kreymborg and Paul Rosenfeld, one of whom is dead now. (I am talking about *their* lack of kindness, justice, or something.)

It seems to me we should talk now. Could you come here and meet Martha and me? Shall I say you and your wife? Is it better if we saw you in New Jersey, in Rutherford? All this is not the most important thing.

As I see it, the most important thing is, that I properly honor the ethical and poetic meaning of your statements. It is a matter of center meeting center.

Would you like Martha to send you my talk on "Poetry and Technique," the one I mentioned?

And this I see, too.

One. If you want to give a reading of my poems, why, surely, do so.

Two. Your letter can be used with publishers to give my poems greater circulation. I hope you see this as good.

I know that I want to be considerate of you. I have said your letter affected me deeply, and went deeply into me. I want to honor the cause of it. I respect life, personality, you.

The Poetry Group, which I teach, has been coming to see my poems better. I had thought, that through various persons seeing my poems truly and honestly, they would reach others. Of course, this can still be so. Would you like to be at a meeting of the Poetry Group here? It is honest, sober, no vanity-flummery.

There is the question of Aesthetic Realism. This arises from the poetry. It is the logic of poetry. It is the ethics of poetry. Aesthetic Realism is aesthetics in the big sense, and it is how real.

I have a fear of cluttering things. However, I do think it would be good to see how poetry and human beings go together in my pamphlet published by the Society, called *The Aesthetic Method in Self-Conflict*.

These things then arise:

1. Yes, to a reading of my poems.
2. Wouldn't publishers be much affected by your letter, rightly affected?

3. Shouldn't we meet here or in New Jersey?
4. Couldn't my talk on "Poetry and Technique" stand for some of my sentiments about technique?
5. Wouldn't it be good to see how poetry evolves into a way of seeing people? Does this happen in the pamphlet *The Aesthetic Method in Self-Conflict?*

I begin now Part Two of this letter. Aesthetic Realism does arise from poetry. That is why I have thought it proper to have letterheads with the words Aesthetic Realism on top. I think you would love Aesthetic Realism, as a friend to poetry.

The words in your letter come from such a deep place they terrify. How one person understands another is a terrifying matter.

And Aesthetic Realism is for the purpose of persons understanding persons.

I have made some requests of you, stated and implied. Perhaps you can make some of me.

Next week I talk on my poems again. Your letter has jolted the Poetry Group of Aesthetic Realism, in a mighty and fine way.

If you take a long time answering this, we'll likely send you "Poetry and Technique" anyway. And honoring you, we shall go ahead affected by one of the most lovely and amazing documents ever.

Al que quiere.

Request of Oneself

William Carlos Williams
Is a person;

W. C. Williams
Is reality.
Let this mean all it can
And should and must and will
To me.

So long a while.

Sincerely,
ELI SIEGEL

FROM MARTHA BAIRD'S 1951 JOURNAL

Monday, December 17. We had a second letter from Williams which was encouraging. He asked for more of the poems, said he'd given the ones he had to a man from the Golden Goose Press of Ohio; said he's arranging some kind of poetry reading at the Museum of Modern Art and is thinking of having three poets read for twenty minutes each, and if he does this, would ES like to read "Montana" there? Said he and his wife would like to come to the Poetry Group some time in January, except the 11th. Said he distrusts the term "Aesthetic Realism," feels "The Poem" is the best term. Said he'd rather see ES write than reason about writing.

This is what E. most fears: that people who see him as logical can't see him as poetic, and people who see him as poetic can't see him as logical—and he has to be both. We were going to send Williams the "Poetry and Technique" lecture—I typed it especially; but now we hesitate. We also hesitate about the Poetry Group and think maybe it would be better for them to come just to visit us first.

ELI SIEGEL TO W. C. WILLIAMS

January 3, 1952

Dear William Carlos Williams:

I have thought of how best we could meet. Certainly, I should like you to visit a meeting of the Poetry Group. But then the idea of my talking for an hour or more, with you passive, has not seemed so right to me. Besides, it would be one of those expository things. You want your poetry straight.

Martha is sending you a copy of "Poetry and Technique," which is from a recording of a talk I gave in 1948. This will give you an idea of what has been happening some Wednesdays.

I hope the following arrangement will suit you. Our "day off" is Thursday. Perhaps you and your wife could come here on Thursday, January 24, about 8 P.M. At this time we could all meet, and say things to each other. On Wednesday, January 30, I shall talk on "Poetry Looked At." This is a talk meant to place Poetry among all the Arts. However, if you choose, you and your wife are invited to come on this evening of January 30, just so. I should like the Thursday preliminary, and in order to bring it about, the Wednesday visit could be made later. As they say, there are problems in everything.

What this boils down to is this: Will you be our guests at a meeting of the Poetry Group, Wednesday, January 30, 8:30? Optionally, et cetera, could you visit us—as a warming up occasion, Thursday, January 24?

The Poetry Group, as I said, are honest persons trying to place poetry within life. A few are definitely "literary." Some are chiefly interested in arts like sculpture and painting.

I have taken some time answering your letter because I wanted to give full consideration to the matter of our meeting.

So 1952 has begun with a poetry-time problem.

So I shall read "Hot Afternoons Have Been in Montana" on March 26.

Do let 1952 please you profoundly.

I hope you find no clutter in this letter: just sweetness and a desire to be accurate. If confusion about time-tables seems to be present, it's the fault of a molecular but none-the-less estimably trying universe.

Greetings, esteem and greetings.

Sincerely,

ELI SIEGEL

FROM MARTHA BAIRD'S 1952 JOURNAL

Sunday, January 13. More correspondence with Williams. He has definitely asked ES to read "Montana" at the Museum of Modern Art on March 26, and they are supposed to come January 24, Thursday, "weather permitting." We sent them a note, confirming the date, and explaining about 3-C and 5-B.

FROM THE SIEGELS TO THE WILLIAMSES

January 9, 1952

Dear Dr. and Mrs. Williams:

So we shall expect you on Thursday, January 24, at 8 P.M.

The bell to ring is M. Baird, 3-C. 3-C (one flight up,

to the right) faces you as you come up the courtyard. We also live at 5-B, marked Eli Siegel. Housing in New York led to this.

It is good all these things are in motion. And let there be good "informal" things, and good formal things.

Long live Poetry, Architecture, and Geography.

Long live Paterson and syllables.

Greetings forever.

MARTHA BAIRD, ELI SIEGEL

FROM MARTHA BAIRD'S 1952 JOURNAL

Thursday, January 24. It is the day of Williams' visit. For two days I have been hearing weather reports nervously, fearing a blizzard. Today is bright and clear and cold. I am less nervous since reading his poems. Yesterday and today I read the whole 1934 *Collected Poems.* A lot of them I don't understand, but they are all alive, and many things hit me very much. In "The Descent of Winter," these lines about old people are very kind:

> Their feet hurt, they are weak
> they should not have to suffer
> as younger people must and do—
> there should be a truce for them.

And there is one on the cord of a windowshade, seen so sharply and with so much meaning, on "The Red Wheelbarrow" principle. And these lines about "The Red Lily":

You are, upon

your steady stem
one trumpeted wide flower

And then he says:

in your common cup
all beauty lies.

I can also see from these poems why ES's might affect him so much. ES seems to start from the whole world and get it into one thing; Williams starts with one thing, and when he is on the ball, the whole world spreads out from it. But it seems to me his poems are not sure of themselves, and sometimes they get splintery. But he is Somebody, and I think about him. Why should this one person, out of all those born in New Jersey, why should he have all this going on in his head, and this drive to put it down, make poems of it? It is like the feeling I had about Stendhal: how did *he* get to know all this? E. says this is the mystery of the artistic mind. One could ask the same question about him. In his letter, Williams did ask it: how did *he* come to all this?

So it is Thursday, The Day, and I am nervous. I ask E. what we should talk about. He says, "We'll see. It depends on how he is."

We have dinner, and E. listens to *all* the news broadcasts, four in a row. I don't know if he listens, but he has them on.

Then it is 8 o'clock, and I, with my pessimism, wonder if we'll just sit here and wait and nobody'll come. Shame! It is not two minutes, and the bell rings.

There he is, an elderly gentleman, with glasses, looking like his picture, with a young woman who, he says, is Mrs. Williams. This is confusing, and I wonder if he has gotten married again since his autobiography, because surely this can't be Flossie whom he married in 1912. It turns out she is his daughter-in-law, Virginia, married to his son Paul, who is in "the retail trade with Abraham and Straus."

He is nice. He surpasses my fondest hopes. He is honest. He wants to see things. He says, "Yes, god-damnit, I want to be conscious till the very last flicker!" He listens. He says, "I'm a damn good listener." He gets in these damns, but they are rather like punctuation than curses, and the impression one gets of him is of nakedness and innocence. It is curious that he should be so innocent, he has certainly been through plenty; but it is right that he is. E. has that quality too. I remember once someone described his voice as "naked," and I felt it was right. It means not all covered up with something else, something extraneous.

E. tells him I read his autobiography and am not sure about his taste. He is referring to taste in liquor, but Williams thinks he means taste in general. This is corrected later. So we have the scotch. He says he doesn't care anything about liquor, he gets drunk on the imagination. The only thing liquor does for him, if he gets too much, is make him amorous and make a damn fool of himself.

E. asks what he thought of the technique lecture. He says he hasn't studied it. He looked at it, but he can't give any formed opinion. Then he says he never got the second bunch of poems we sent him, and later it is not clear that he ever got the technique lecture either. Anyway, we give him some more poems.

E. asks him if any of the poems besides "Montana" stood out. He says he doesn't remember, but he read the first group (he didn't get to the second group) and he thought, "This is good stuff!" And he liked these better than the poem we sent later. (This was the "Marriage Poem.") Then he started to write that letter, he says, and he didn't mean it to be so long, but he started writing it, and as he wrote, what he had seen got clearer, and that was the highpoint of his seeing.

E. says he feels that letter would impress publishers, the way it comes, so right from the heart, and with the respect for Williams' opinion that is had nowadays; but he wants Williams to be sure it wouldn't be used in any superficial way. Williams says, how could it be, it's about the poems, isn't it? He says sure we can use it.

He is proud of that letter and says later—though he's against criticism as a general thing and thinks the poet ought to spend his time writing poems— later he says maybe that letter is a work of art itself. E. says it is an important document in American literature. Williams agrees.

Williams says he wants to *see*, and he wants to say what he sees, and he wants to get at the mystery of technique in terms of the *line*. E. asks if he thinks he'll ever see what he wants to? He says no, not in his lifetime. He thinks the artists are working slowly, slowly, and a little at a time something is added, and maybe in five hundred years it'll be, but this is not the time. He says if Shakespeare had been born twenty years later, he couldn't have done what he did: the conditions wouldn't have been right.

E. shows him the books we have of his: *In the American Grain*. Williams says that was a damn good book, it's too bad it didn't sell. E. says, yes, but it is uneven. Williams says, yes, it is uneven, but it is a good book. Also we have *Kora in Hell*, a rare early book. W. says he has never read from this when he does readings but he thinks sometime he may. He thinks now it's sort of juvenile. He says this boyishly. He is nice.

He says he's been invited to read at Princeton, after all these years. He's rather miffed at Princeton. There it is, right in New Jersey, and he's been invited to colleges all over the country but never to Princeton. Finally last year he was invited, but he wasn't very eager, and told them he was busy. This year, they invited him again. They told him it would only be $100—that's all they have for that sort of thing. W. says that's ridiculous—Princeton only has $100! Anyway, he's going to do it and get his $100, but he's not going to knock himself out.

Talking about technique, E. says there are two ways of looking at it, as at a wound. Say a man has a wound in his arm. You can see it as a specific thing—this is Williams' way; and you can see it as having to do with man's whole organism and with organism in general. This, he implies, is more his way. To show what he means, he has me read some from *The Aesthetic Method* about the Shelley line. Williams is interested in this, and we give him a copy of this too.

Something comes up about D. H. Lawrence. E.

says Lawrence and Eliot aren't poets, but Williams is. The daughter-in-law, Ginny, says she thinks Lawrence is a beautiful poet, and she was under the impression Williams thought so, too. Williams says no, he doesn't think Lawrence was a poet, but he feels his general position in literature wasn't appreciated. (Ginny doesn't say much, but she is nice too, and not pretentious. She helps me with the scotch. I don't say much either.)

E. talks about Lawrence in a way that seems to hit Williams very much. E. says he had a fight between the organic and the intellectual, and he couldn't make sense of it; and this, in a way, is what killed him; and that in being too much for him, you are being for what was his enemy. Then he says some things about sex, how it is a form of knowing. This hits Williams, and he says yes, he wants to be aware of everything. People want to be dissolved, as in the ocean, but this isn't good, and he wants to be conscious "to the very last flicker."

Then Williams says some things about the French. The French, he thinks, are perfectly at ease about this. Take Baudelaire—go live with a whore if you want. Or the way they are now about homosexuals—go ahead, if you want. He shakes his head, as if he couldn't approve of this, and yet he seems to be envious of those who do. E. says the French are just like everybody else, and when it comes down to it, Williams is more at ease than Baudelaire. He should read "My Heart Laid Bare." Williams seems incredulous, but pleased.

Another thing that pleases him is when E. says

he'd like to talk about Williams' poems so as to have Williams love them more. W. says he'd like to come to the Poetry Group. E. asks W. if he'd like him to talk about *his* poems. Oh, he would. So we get the calendar, and arrange it to be on March 5. This is three weeks before the Museum of Modern Art reading. He doesn't want E. to waste his time being a critic, but he wants to hear about *his* poems. I think of the times E. has talked about Coleridge and Shakespeare and how I have wished so much they could hear it, and Williams will have the chance.

About the MOMA reading, he says Lloyd Frankenberg told him it was a "stroke of genius" to have E. read there. E. hoots delightedly at this. Frankenberg, I gather, is one of those literary people with whom he hasn't gotten on well. Williams says Untermeyer may be there too, and he also thinks having E. is a stroke of genius. We both hoot delightedly. E. says Williams has performed a miracle, to cut through all that. He says he had about given up the literary people, and he guesses they have given him up too. Williams says, But you are remembered. He says it is too bad E. hasn't put himself forth more. E. asks if he thinks it's for a good reason or a bad one? Williams says a good one, he thinks. E. says he's not sure. Williams says, well, it's been E.'s choice, and he respects it.

There is talk about the general. Williams is very shy of what he calls philosophy. I think he associates it with stuffiness and fraud. He says he likes the general *in* the specific. He doesn't even want to talk about *poetry*, he wants to use the word *poem*. E. says

W. is afraid if he liked the general, he'd have to hate the specific; but, truly, if he loved the general, he'd love the specific more.

E. talks about the way he sees things and he uses the word *burden*. Williams says, "It's not a burden, man, it's a privilege!" E. says it is a privilege, but it is also a burden. Ginny says, "But poetry is for pleasure!" Comparing his and Williams' lives, E. says they have both been through things, and for Williams in a way it has been easier, and in a way it has been harder.

Well, it is a most pleasant visit. It is really enjoyable. No one is uncomfortable. No one is looking anybody over or sizing anybody up. There is real talk, and it is not hurried; and though so much is left out, much, much is said. It is as lovely a time as I can remember having.

They have to get a 10:15 train on the other side of the river, and just before they go, E. reads to them "Montana." Oh, does he read it! Williams cannot contain himself. "Oh," he says, "great!"

We put on our coats too, and walk with them down Hudson Street to Christopher, where they get the Tubes to New Jersey. E. walks with Ginny, and I walk with Dr. Williams.

He tells me he can't walk so fast. I say I can't walk so fast either, on account of my shoes. He says he had a stroke last year, his heart, his brain, everything; and he took six months off from his practice, and his son who is a doctor took over for him. Now his wife wants him to take a winter vacation, and he doesn't want to take a vacation, and besides he doesn't want to spend several hundred dollars that way, with his income cut down; but she says they can afford it. I say, couldn't he take a vacation at home? He says yes, he could take a wonderful vacation; but she's been a good wife to him. She's stuck to him all these years, and being married to a person who is practicing medicine and is also a poet isn't easy, he's bound to get himself into trouble.

I ask him if the evening was the way he thought? He implies it was better than he thought it would be. I ask if he was scared? I was. Was he scared he'd be disappointed? No, he says, not that, but he thought maybe it would be stuffy. He didn't think he'd be disappointed. He knew when he read those poems the person who wrote them was all right. I tell him E. is an artist all the time, that is the way he sees things all the time.

We say good-night, and they go down the stairs to the train, and we go home.

Friday, January 25. At the Friday class, ES makes a little statement—I wish I had recorded it to copy. He says we were visited by William Carlos Williams and that he showed himself to be "deeply likable" and one of the few persons who got a whiff of the meaning of what goes on here and didn't get scared and run away. Then he says, very plainly, and so sweetly, "I am not going to use him; in fact, if there is to be anything like that, it will be more the other way." And he says Williams may come to the Poetry Group.

Then he gives a talk about Weariness and Energy, and Daniel Webster, Judy Garland, the sun, and Shelley.

Saturday, January 26. Thinking of Williams, I remember a few things I forgot to put down. Early in the evening, E. asked him if he thought the world was good, or that being interested in it—and Williams certainly is interested—implied feeling it was good? Williams thought about this and he said, "Yes, it is good," very emphatically.

When he said he didn't like the "Marriage Poem" as much as the others, he said it simply, with no hesitation or explanations, the way you can say something like that when you are sure of your good will and of the other person's sense of it.

He said something about people that was rather complicated, and when he had finished, E. said, "In other words, you are saying you have been hurt by people." And he said, "Oh, hell, yes."

Also he talked of how people are lonesome, and each one is shut up in his own group of cells. And E., referring to possible feelings of apprehension about his coming here, said "there is always the fear of not being comprehended," and Williams nodded.

Thoughts of dying are much on his mind. I have seen this in his writing. But he said that sometimes at night he lies awake thinking about whether to be buried or cremated—things like that. He does seem kind of fragile. He is thin. He is energetic and very wide awake, but there seems to be something frail.

He described very well the feeling in writing a poem, as if you had two horses, and they're running, and they're wild, but you have them under control. And he makes the gesture, as if he had the reins in his hands, and he sits on the edge of the couch, and his face is all alight.

E., talking of Williams' poems, used the word "unsure"—either that the poems are unsure or that W. is unsure of them. He agreed very readily. I was surprised. Also E. said there is a great love of things in the poems, and also a fear of things.

E. told him all the poems of his he has talked on, and he reminded him of a critical article W. had written which he had forgotten. He was pleased by this.

Talking about technique, E. used the term "free verse." Williams looked surprised. E. said, Well, after all, that's what he writes. He said in free verse, you go from disorder to order (I think this is where W. made the simile about the horses), and in other verse you start with order and get to disorder, but it comes to the same thing: you have to have both.

Wednesday, January 30. We get the announcement from the Museum of Modern Art. It has "March 26, New Poets Introduced by William Carlos Williams: Stanley Lawrence Berne, David Lougee, Harold Norse, Kenneth Beaudoin, Eli Siegel."

E. is much taken with being called a "New Poet." I thought he might object, but he says no, he rather likes it.

The paradoxes of his career are something staggering. He says he almost feels as if it were 1924 again. He wrote "Montana" on February 10, 1924. He says every year since 1922 somebody has talked of him in terms of superlatives, and quite spontaneously. And then also there has been all the disparagement.

ELI SIEGEL TO W. C. WILLIAMS

February 14, 1952

Dear Williams (Bill):

I hope these weeks have been as good as weeks can be. This is a poetic and definite wish.

You know, we agreed that I talk on your poems, etc., here on March 5, Wednesday, 8:30. Do you still see this as likable? I hope you do, but if you don't, or want to postpone the time, let us know. We do have an abhorrence of having you do anything that makes for constraint, or absence of adequate pleasedness.

If the time still seems all right to you, will you please tell us so. We shall then announce it to persons in the Poetry Group and others. Also, perhaps you could mention some people we could inform rightly; and invite to come. Put differently, is there anyone you'd like to come whom we might notify?

Furthermore, if you have any notions about how the talk best could be, I should like you to mention them. My aim is to honor the truth, honor and please you deeply, and be accurate to everything else. The talk I mean to be a large, deep experience in truth and meaning, pleasing to the Muses, just to sound and picture, welcome and right and authentic to Williams.

We have got, through a member of the Society who gets the Museum of Modern Art announcements, a copy of the announcement containing the event of March 26. We sent for more copies, and got them.

Good voyaging.—Do you like the New Directions issue of your poems?—There is a poem of yours translated into the French by Eugène Jolas (in his *Anthologie de la nouvelle poésie américaine*: Paris, 1928) called *"Portrait de l'auteur."* I do not remember to have seen this in English, but in the French—or I dare say any language—it says a lot. I am now after the original English. You say, in French, in this poem:

> *Prends-moi dans tes bras, dis-moi la chose*
> *   la plus ordinaire*
> *qui soit dans ton esprit,*
> *dis n'importe quoi. Je te comprendrai!—*
> *C'est la folie des feuilles des bouleaux*
> *   s'ouvrant*
> *froides, une à une.*

How, how! How necessarily beautiful! Quelle pénétration. Quelle compréhension. Quelle, quelle! Quelle amitié à la poésie! Quelle amitié au réalisme aesthétique!

—So, getting back, we hope to resume our communication. Regards to Ginny.

Sincerely,
ELI SIEGEL

P.S. There is an enclosure expressing the best aspects of Greek or any contentment-and-excitement.

Meant To Be

> Consider, friends, how lovingly,
> One things meets another:
> As for instance, kitten a kitten,
> Leaf a leaf,

Book a book,
Or planet a thing.
Consider how this can go on,
Indefinitely, in any time,
Let alone all time.
Consider, friends, the impermanence of
    obstruction,
The friendliness and everlastingness of
    possibility,
And such matters:
And you will alter a little
The irritation of long ago,
Question its authenticity,
And use the past
To be refreshed,
As it was meant to be—
Used now.[1]

FROM MARTHA BAIRD'S 1952 JOURNAL

Saturday, February 16. A letter from Williams, so fast! Yes, he says, March 5 stands, and he hopes to bring Ginny. E. asked him if there was anyone he'd like us to invite, and he says Harold Norse, David Gascoyne, and Lloyd Frankenberg. Says the poem E. sent was excellent, and he'd like E. to read it at the MOMA before "Montana," to warm people up. Says he didn't know anything of Eugène Jolas' translation of his poem, was amazed to learn of it.

1. This poem, written the same day as the letter, now appears in *Hot Afternoons Have Been in Montana: Poems*, p. 56.

Sunday, February 17. We have a Society meeting, and ES tells about the March 5 Poetry Group. He says everyone won't be able to come, and thinks priority should go to those who have shown an interest in poetry before now. He says nobody should oh and ah over someone well-known coming here, and they shouldn't even talk about Williams if they don't take the trouble to read some of his poetry. And if they don't like it, they shouldn't come either; he doesn't want any insincerity.

Tuesday, February 19. At lunch time, Lou Dienes brings us brand new copies of Williams' *Collected Earlier Poems* and *Collected Later Poems* which he got from the New Directions warehouse in Brooklyn. E. is studying hard for his talk, and is going to do it thoroughly, as one would suppose.

Then we write letters inviting Mark Van Doren, Untermeyer, and Vivienne Koch to the March 5 talk. Miss Koch has written a critical study on Williams, published by New Directions, according to the dust wrapper on the collected poems.

Wednesday, March 5. At 8:25, Williams arrives. So punctual. Just five minutes early. Ginny is with him, I am glad to see, but she looks rather angry or something—I don't know. Everybody is here but Norse and Gascoyne, so I call E. that they are here, and he comes down.

He comes in with his books, and before I know it, he is in his chair and beginning the talk, and he has a sob in his voice, and I think for a minute he is going to cry.

The sob goes away, and he gives a magnificent talk—covering all Williams' work, and criss-crossing back and forth so that you have a feeling of a central thing going through it all. He is funny too, and I see Williams is nodding his head and laughing. It is over two hours long, and just by luck and the most clever foresight, I have a third spool ready, so it can all be recorded.

2

*Williams' Poetry Talked about
by Eli Siegel,
and William Carlos Williams
Present and Talking:
March 5, 1952*

Part Two

I call this "Williams' Poetry Looked At: A Critical Poem," and I hope you see why.

A short while ago I wrote something, pretty spontaneously, called "Eliot and Williams: A Distinction." As I read this, it isn't because, I think, I'm too much affected by social goings-on, but because, as Dr. Williams himself implies in his work, the honesty of the word has a great deal to do with what's going to happen to us. Aesthetic Realism goes for that honesty, and I was very much moved when Dr. Williams said things which I felt were honest about work of mine.

There are people here who haven't cared for poetry, and we don't pretend around here. But they were learning about poetry as they were learning about themselves, and some people here know more about themselves than most people in America. The thing that in 1924 impelled me to write "Hot Afternoons Have Been in Montana" was the thing which, in Aesthetic Realism, I have been trying to present somewhat more "lucidly," more systematically, and many people here have been affected.

Now when Dr. Williams heard that I was interested in Aesthetic Realism, I imagine he thought, "Well, another poet deviated." I don't think so. I think

I am proving what Dr. Williams says in his *Autobiography*, page 264: "Thinking, talking, writing constantly about the poem as a way of life."[1]

If the poem is a way of life, is that to be taken literarily, or does it mean just that? In Aesthetic Realism, it means just that.

Not only has Dr. Williams said this in prose, he has also said it in poetry. I refer to a poem on page 209 of his *Collected Later Poems*. In this poem, the word is dealt with almost as if it were religion. It is dealt with almost in keeping with the New Testament statement, "In the beginning was the word." (When I was in a gay mood, I said, "In the beginning was the word, and then some back talk.") What Dr. Williams is saying, with a most magnificent iteration, is that the word and the line are a test of honesty and the accurate life. This poem is called "Convivio." It is recent. I'm glad that it's recent.

> . . . the enemy, those
> who despise the word, flout it, stem,
> leaves and root; the liars who decree laws
> with no purpose other than to make a screen
> of them for larceny, murder—for our
> murder, we who salute the word and would
> have it clean, full of sharp movement.[2]

There are many eminent people who do not respect the word. In this poem, Dr. Williams has in mind

1. *The Autobiography of William Carlos Williams* (New York: Random House, 1951).

2. "Convivio," lines 11-16. The whole poem was read. Complete text is in *The Collected Later Poems of William Carlos Williams* (Norfolk, Conn.: New Directions, 1950), p. 209. Page numbers in 1963 edition are the same.

various persons having much power, and they've been around America from the very beginning. But then there are other persons who, without knowing it, don't respect the word and its power, and Dr. Williams, from his *Autobiography*, has known many of them. It is very hard to respect the word; and it is very hard to respect the word in relation to other words. You have to study; and study, it seems, is a secondary thing in the history of the human race.

T. S. Eliot, I have thought, was a person who on the whole did not respect the word. He is not dishonest in the way that a Joseph McCarthy is, but he is not honest enough. It was long before tonight that I wrote a review of Eliot for *Scribner's*; and I wrote of him as a very accomplished, intricate deceiver. I still think so. That's neither here nor there, whether he's a deceiver. The point is that he's not a poet. And one of the most distressing things in America is that people think that T. S. Eliot is a poet. I have found him very interesting—it was nearly thirty years ago that I lectured on *The Waste Land*, in Baltimore, and that shows how interesting I found him; but I came to see that he was no poet. Recently I wrote this short document I mentioned, which I read now:

Eliot and Williams: A Distinction

There are two poets who are affecting minds in America today. One is T. S. Eliot, the other is William Carlos Williams. It is good to see that the effect of the first is waning, and the effect of the second is growing. It is good, because it is just poetically.

So why is it just? It is just, for Eliot, however esteemed, has failed in his work generally to make spontaneity one with structure; and Williams has not failed. Certainly, there have been mishaps in the diverse, numerously-presented work of Williams, but the New Jersey man has shown again and again that seeing as instinct can change into seeing as architecture, organization, logic.

In the work of Eliot, however, and this includes esteemed writings like "Prufrock," *The Waste Land,* and the *Four Quartets,* personal seeing has not just so, not uninterruptedly, not truly and energetically come to have the structure, technique, or form that Eliot uses. As to Williams, though: he has seen, and he has seen in such a way, and saw what he saw in such a way, that again and again, as I have stated, his seeing came to be structure, took on form, changed to musical and visual organization. That is why it is good that Williams is affecting people more, and Eliot rather less.[3]

The review of Eliot that I wrote for *Scribner's* many years ago was set in type, but then it was thought it went too far, and it was changed. It was a review taking up Eliot's poetry and criticism— chiefly his criticism—and I said it was the road towards literary torpor, boredom, semi-death, and death.

The review that I wrote somewhat later of Dr. Williams' work was what was called a "filler." I wrote it passionately. It got in small type in the

3. Expanded into a full-length article and published in the *University of Kansas City Review,* XXII, 1 (Autumn 1955), 41-43. Reprinted in present text, pp. 141-146.

spring of 1934, and those of you who are interested can look it up. I wrote with my frequent abandon, but I meant every vowel of it.

William Carlos Williams: Collected Poems, 1921–1931. Objectivist Press. $2.—

The poems of Williams belong to the history of American Poetry and therefore, Literature. This is not meant to be a highfalutin' statement; it may be wrong but it's careful. Of late, Williams has written inferior things; but a man's work is his whole work. In this book, "The Red Wheelbarrow" is as good as the author says it is: it is mystical, physical, and musical; and gives you a good case of poetic shivers. And many other things of Williams get to heaven and caves at once. Again carefully: in the person of William Carlos Williams of Rutherford, N. J., now with us, we have a better poet than Henry Wadsworth Longfellow or James Russell Lowell. Williams is big time—any time in American Poetry.[4]

Since then, as I intimated in the first document I read, Dr. Williams has come to be the leading poetic influence, perhaps, in America. To show that this is not simply a way of hailing a guest, I read from the work on Dr. Williams by Vivienne Koch. Miss Koch is quoting René Taupin; he wrote a book on the influence of the French symbolists on American poets. My own feeling is that the influence of the French symbolists on Dr. Williams tends towards the scant. However, these statements are interesting:

4. *Scribner's,* XCV, 4 (April 1934), 24. Unsigned.

> Ranking Williams as one of the three greatest American poets, M. Taupin raises the question, "Perhaps Williams has composed the formula for American art?"

And another quotation from Taupin:

> "Williams knows more about the poetic imagination than any American poet today."[5]

There is no doubt that M. Taupin's work, *L'Influence du symbolisme français sur la poésie américaine,* which appeared in 1929 and which was later translated, helped to place the work of Williams. However, even in the appreciation of Williams, there may be things missing.

I see him as representing organized and subtle joy. Sometimes there is a tendency to deal with Dr. Williams as if he were some very abstruse architecture. That is to be found in the work of Miss Koch. I think that poetry has as its purpose a good time that you can be proud of eternally. All the structure goes for a proud good time, a good time that arises out of accuracy. In Dr. Williams' work there is a great deal about what is really a good time. The very last passage of *Paterson* is about that, and there are many passages about what is a good time. This passage, by the way, is one of the very best in *Paterson:*

> A large, compact bitch gets up, black,
> from where she has been lying

5. Quoted by Vivienne Koch, *William Carlos Williams* (Norfolk, Conn.: New Directions, 1950), p. 32.

under the bank, yawns and stretches with
a half suppressed half whine, half cry   .

. . . .
                    Climbing the
bank, after a few tries, he picked
some beach plums from a low bush and
sampled one of them, spitting the seed out,
then headed inland, followed by the dog[6]

I cannot deal with *Paterson* extensively now, but
the whole poem is about disorganized good times and
disorganized feelings, and the poem is an attempt—
as everything, in a sense, is an attempt—of Dr.
Williams to show that chaos has its symmetry, that
the uncertain has its rightness, and that the God-
damnedest awful mishmash somewhere has sense to
it. It's a very noble purpose. And the distinction of
Dr. Williams is that when he tackles mishmash, it's
really mishmash.

There is something—and I hope to show that this
is so—continuous in the work of Dr. Williams from
about 1909 on, through the book that is fairly current
(hard to get) *The Tempers* of 1913, and then the
Al que quiere, the *Kora in Hell,* the *Sour Grapes,* the
Spring and All, and so on, until we come to the collected poems. There is something continuous.

And one aspect of this something continuous is the
desire to meet the chaotic, the repellent, the ugly.

I have just now made a statement about Eliot and
Williams. Eliot in *The Waste Land* came to a resounding success, one of the most resounding successes in

6. *Paterson* (Norfolk, Conn.: New Directions, 1948), pp. 237-
238. Page numbers in 1963 edition are the same. The entire
passage was read.

non-popular poetry. Eliot is not popular in the way that we can say Ella Wheeler Wilcox was once popular, or Edgar Guest, or to take a person who does belong to poetry, Carl Sandburg. But Eliot did affect people by saying that the world was run down and it was one big job for the street cleaners. That is in *The Waste Land*.

It is interesting that perhaps the earliest important review in book form (that I have seen) of Williams' work makes the comparison that I made a short while ago. Ezra Pound, as those of you who know Williams' *Autobiography* know well, was a person who went after his education while Dr. Williams was going after his. Pound tried to conduct an orchestra and Dr. Williams tried to find out how body behaves in New Jersey. I'm reading from Pound's *Instigations*, published in 1920 (and, by the way, it's one of the worst printed books I've ever seen—Boni and Liveright, 1920). But Pound got into book form quite early. While Dr. Williams was being printed by the Four Seas Company of Boston, Pound was being printed by Knopf. There's a difference. I read the review of Williams by Pound. It is still right, and it is interesting that there is a comparison of Williams and Eliot.

Mina Loy isn't very much around. Marianne Moore, whom Pound reviews, is very much around. Eliot is very much around. I must say, after being careful, I do not see Miss Moore as a poet, I have not seen Miss Loy as a poet, and I haven't seen Mr. Eliot as a poet. It is interesting, what Pound says of these two ladies and the two men. I am reading now from a section of *Instigations* by Ezra Pound, called "In the Vortex," and the subsection is "The New Poetry":

Distinct and as different as possible from the orderly statements of Eliot, and from the slightly
acid whimsicalities of these ladies, are the poems
of Carlos Williams. If the sinuosities and mental
quirks of Misses Moore and Loy are difficult to
follow I do not know what is to be said for some of
Mr. Williams' ramifications and abruptnesses. I do
not pretend to follow all of his volts, jerks, sulks,
balks, outblurts and jump-overs; but for all his
roughness there remains with me the conviction
that there is nothing meaningless in his book, *Al
que quiere,* not a line. There is whimsicality as we
found it in his earlier poems: *The Tempers* (published by Elkin Mathews), in the verse to "The
Coroner's Children," for example. There is distinct-
ness and color, as was shown in his "Postlude," in
Des Imagistes; but there is beyond these qualities
the absolute conviction of a man with his feet on
the soil, on a soil personally and peculiarly his own.
He is rooted. He is at times almost inarticulate,
but he is never dry, never without sap in abundance.[7]

Well, as far as I can see, Mr. Eliot in these thirty
years and more, still hasn't got "sap." And there are
lots of people, some of whom apparently take Dr.
Williams as a guide, who also have a lot of structure,
but they don't have what the maple tree has. They
don't have juice. They don't have the energy. They
don't have the something which Dr. Williams talks of
again and again, the thing that makes a flower shoot
out of the ground, ramify, take on radiation, take on

7. Ezra Pound, *Instigations* (New York: Boni and Liveright,
1920), p. 241.

form; which makes a tree get to twigs. They don't have that. They are mighty little like a tree.

This is shown in a matter which, as I said, interests Williams very much: the nature of the word, the nature of the line. I have been interested in that very much too, and I have always thought that the line is the essential thing in poetry. It is a certain thrust that corresponds to a thrust in the world itself. I don't want to be portentous, but I think that criticism which deals fully with the line will have a great deal to do with physics, not so much with "psychology," in the collegiate sense.

The line is something Williams has always been interested in. It happens to be an organic thrust. It happens to be a combination of hardness and softness, swiftness and slowness, the visual and the musical, the spacious and the concentrated; and it is shown in what happens to the syllables, the vowels, the consonants, the kind of word used, the rubbing of one word against another, and the landscape of the line— the hills, the plains, the ditches, the chasms, the cliffs, the whole geography in the line.

I do say the nature of the line has something to do with the present quantum theory. A quantum in its simplest definition is: "a unit of energy corresponding to the atom in the atomic theory." But the important thing about it is that it isn't a flowing thing, it is something that jumps, there is mutation in it. Motion is of two kinds. Dr. Williams has written of both kinds. He says somewhere that there is the motion of a "pickaninny"; and then there is the motion which is gliding. Well, that is true. The kangaroo and the snake should both get into a line of poetry. A good line welcomes both.

The quantum theory has something to do with this, and I read now the more complicated definition from Funk and Wagnalls' *Practical Standard Dictionary:*

Quantum theory (Theoretical Physics), the theory deduced by Planck that radiation by any body is an interrupted process, each radiator emitting energy in equal amounts termed *quanta,* the value of which depend on a universal constant and the frequency of the vibrations of the radiators.[8]

The distinction of Dr. Williams' work is that his lines very often have the surprising and also right quality that energy shown in any field of matter whatsoever has. And when we see it attended by the emotions of a person, we get to something important.

However, it is well to deal with the line a little more closely. One of the books I've had for a fairly long time is one of the anthologies in which Williams appeared, *Others,* 1916; and he appeared in the other *Others.* Among the people present in the *Others* of 1916 happen to be Wallace Stevens, Eliot with "Portrait of a Lady," Marianne Moore, Carl Sandburg, Ezra Pound; people less known now like Helen Hoyt, the Englishman Douglas Goldring; and persons who are around in other fields—there is the art collector Arensberg, there is the musical critic Pitts Sanborn,

8. *The Practical Standard Dictionary of the English Language* (New York and London: Funk & Wagnalls Company, 1938).

there is the sculptor, apparently, William Zorach; and
there are others. Others, yes.

This is a rather representative showing of what
free verse was doing in America in 1916. Free verse
did have some of its cause in the French vers libre.
But free verse is like money, good and bad; and it
is important to see why free verse is good or bad.
The term is not in such good odor now. There was a
time when it was said that all the radicals in verse
were turning to the sonnet, and they would soon be
writing the chant royal. Dr. Williams, by the way,
has had a campaign against the sonnet for years—I
must say I pity it a little.

But I'd like to deal with the line, and I can't of
course quote too much. There is a poem here by
Kreymborg which was very popular, and I remember
many years ago a person reading it so that he got
the whole room into his sigh. It is likable. I can
say in advance that the trouble with the poem is that
its lines are too softy-soft, they undulate too much,
they are floppy curvedly, sighingly. (I'm talking now
the way Lincoln Gillespie used to talk.) Well, this is
"Vista," of Alfred Kreymborg:

> The snow,
> ah yes, ah yes indeed,
> is white and beautiful, white and beautiful,
> verily beautiful—
> from my window.
> The sea,
> ah yes, ah yes indeed,
> is green and alluring, green and alluring,
> verily alluring—

from the shore.
Love,
ah yes, ah yes, ah yes indeed,
verily yes, ah yes indeed!

I wouldn't say for a moment that that poem couldn't interest people, but it is too much like what I'd call a sagging mattress: it doesn't have firmness. The trouble with free verse lines is that they either get too much like overripe pomegranates or sagging mattresses; or then occasionally they get too much like tightly packed crates, or at the worst like a poker with ridges. This is not the way it should be.

I also must say that Ezra Pound, though I esteem his statement about Williams, is likewise not a master of free verse. I do not see him as a poet. I see his best work as being that very popular "Doria":

> Be in me as the eternal moods
>   of the bleak wind, and not
> As transient things are—
>   gaiety of flowers.

And so on. It's very short—I've said one-third of it. And then the translations from the Chinese. There are things from the *Cantos* that are interesting; but generally he's not a poet because he doesn't know when to be harsh and he doesn't know when to be soft, and he's tried to be harsh and sour and Lord knows what all.

There was a poem of his which was very popular and which Dr. Williams mentions indirectly in his *Autobiography*, called "Shop Girl." And it was very much liked, because there are very few poems of five lines that have in them three poets. Well, I don't see it as great shakes. I read it many years ago—I believe it appeared in *Lustra*—around 1919, as early as that, but I still don't see it as great shakes. I must say, I thought more of it in 1919 than I do now. Yet there is a tendency not to make distinctions; that has always been so.

We come now to Eliot. I do not see Eliot as an artist in verse. I say this very carefully. I have found "Prufrock" and *The Waste Land* interesting, but the man is not a poet. It would be very good if people saw it. There is a poem after *The Waste Land* called "The Hollow Men." I consider it as poetry essentially dull. But talking about its lines—there is a rigidity, there is no flow, and there is no impetus. Mr. Eliot is very different from a fountain. Well, this is section four of "The Hollow Men," and I'll read it as well as I can:

The eyes are not here
There are no eyes here
In this valley of dying stars
In this hollow valley
This broken jaw of our lost kingdoms

In this last of meeting places
We grope together
And avoid speech
Gathered on this beach of the tumid river

Sightless, unless
The eyes reappear

As the perpetual star
Multifoliate rose
Of death's twilight kingdom
The hope only
Of empty men.

As an animal in one of Dr. Williams' poems, "The
Sea-Elephant," would say, "Blouaugh!"

We come now to something of a distinction. Dr.
Williams is not one of the enamored of rhyme.
Hardly. There is some rhymed verse in his collected
poems, but there is very little of it. I have felt that
free verse is a very good thing, and it is the hardest
thing, on the whole, to write. Good free verse is
a harder thing to write than a sonnet or a ballade,
or a chant royal, or a cinquain, or anything else;
it is harder to write even than the Spenserian stanza.
But, for example, Dr. Williams is very much interested
in Villon. Villon is anything but free verse. He has
those continuous rhymes in his ballades, and there's
a refrain, and the whole apparatus of fifteenth-century
French verse. There is also, it seems, a liking for Poe.
Poe is very different from Williams, yet Poe is a
poet, and I have a tendency still to like that barroom
favorite, "The Raven." I don't think it's just by chance
that Mallarmé translated it.

In *In the American Grain*, Dr. Williams says that
"To One in Paradise" is Poe's best poem; he says
this in the last line of his essay on Poe. There is
something in Poe, and there is poetry in "To One in
Paradise." I don't think there is tremendously much,
but there is a good deal. And we have in Poe a man
who carefully rhymed, in fact, he is the greatest

master of what Emerson would call the jingle—
though Emerson was unfair. The last stanza of "To
One in Paradise" is *rhyme;* it's very different from
Dr. Williams' "By the road to the contagious hos-
ital." Yet it is poetry. I'll read that stanza:

> And all my days are trances,
> And all my nightly dreams
> Are where thy gray eye glances,
> And where thy footstep gleams—
> In what ethereal dances,
> By what eternal streams.

Very likable. Very likable, but I think there are some
poems by Williams that are better than "To One
in Paradise."

Now getting to Williams' work. I always like to
read from early editions if possible, and there are
many poems to read; many, many. I'm going to read
in certain instances just a few lines. And I'm going
to begin with the *Others,* from which I read poems
by Kreymborg and Ezra Pound. One of Williams'
most popular poems, "Tract," is here. I talked on
that poem, some of you may remember, some years
ago. But as one listens to the lines again, one gets
that feeling of firmness and flexibility, of casualness
and directness, of the roundabout and the straight
line, which help to make a line.

So these are the first lines of "Tract":

> I will teach you
> my townspeople
> how to perform
> a funeral—

> for you have it
> over a troop
> of artists—
> unless one should
> scour the world—
> you have the ground sense
> necessary.[9]

There is a certain arrangement of words. There is the slang, "you have it over"; there is the word "artists," and "ground sense" and "necessary." There is a subtle, chemical mingling of surprising proprieties in those lines, and in the line, and, one may say, in the word. There is also the sound of speech.

Dr. Williams has written in various styles, particularly in prose. And it is interesting to see that the sound of speech is in a much later work. There is a story about Dago in *Make Light of It*. The sounds used there sometimes, taken out of the paragraph and put into line form, would make for a poem. This Dago is a big rebel, he's Patrick Henry to the nth power. He doesn't want to do anything other people are doing. And he gets into trouble. This, from the story called "An Old Time Raid" in *Make Light of It* (it first appeared in *The Knife of the Times*), is good lingo:

You weren't allowed to smoke. They had big cards hanging down from the ceiling on strings—or wires

9. *Others*, ed. Alfred Kreymborg (New York: Knopf, 1916), p. 136. Also in *The Collected Earlier Poems of William Carlos Williams* (Norfolk, Conn.: New Directions, 1951), p. 129. Here Williams changed the line structure, making six lines of these eleven.

—I dunno. No smoking. There was one right in front of us. This probably gave Dago the idea. He got out a cigar and started to light up.[10]

Well, there are ups and downs in that! And you could arrange it to make a poem. It would be very perky.

When a group of words seem to have a life among themselves, and in being different they seem to say they are friendly in the same way a group of hills and valleys and bushes might—we have something corresponding to the line. And as I said, it corresponds to what quanta are.

But getting back to the work. Another poem of Williams that has remained and is well known and is reaching new audiences now, is the "Pastoral." I'll read the first lines there:

> The little sparrows
> hop ingenuously
> about the pavement
> quarreling
> with sharp voices
> over those things
> that interest them.[11]

The reason for that's being good is the fact that there are these two aspects of the world: the effervescence of it, the manyness of it, the multitudinousness of it, is related to something quiet and inclusive; and it can be a sinister quietness. We have "The little

10. *Make Light of It* (New York: Random House, 1950), p. 30.
11. *Others*, p. 133. *CEP*, p. 124.

sparrows"—that's a fact, they're little. And sometimes a simple fact makes for a good effect. I think one of the most poetic lines in America is: "The short guy in a derby."

There's a change: you have "The little sparrows" and then "hop ingenuously." That's a fancy word, I wouldn't call it one of the words in Basic English, but there's a feeling of the noise of the sparrows in it. "Hop ingenuously"—it's very swift. "About the pavement"—"quarreling"—"with sharp voices"—and you feel that insistence, that expostulation of the sparrows. The way they argue with each other! And you feel that in the way the words are used. I could go further, but this is not a time to linger on one poem. I just want to say this is honest dealing with words. And as I have said, before ethics can come, people have to take words with love and accuracy. Love must always be accuracy.

In the poem there is a comparison:

> But we who are wiser
> shut ourselves in
> on either hand
> and no one knows
> whether we think good
> or evil.[12]

There's an interesting comparison between something quite still and something in a delicate uproar. More could be said of this.

Anyway, those two poems, "Tract" and "Pastoral," belong to poetry. This is no time to make for com-

12. "Pastoral," lines 8-13.

petition, but it is a time for distinction. The source of those two poems is different from the source of poems by people like Eliot, and MacLeish, and Robinson Jeffers, and most of the work of Edwin Arlington Robinson, and I'm afraid a good many of the English persons. I do not see, as I have said, Spender as a poet, or Auden—I've tried. I don't see it. They don't have the organized volcano.

Proceeding, we get to a poem which is about poetry itself. Williams has written often of trees and flowers. He has written of all the things that happen in that locality he writes about, and most things happening in America happen in New Jersey. There's not the Grand Canyon, but most other things are there. I get to a poem now which here is included as having appeared first in the *Collected Poems* of 1934, "Young Sycamore."

This is a poem about how spontaneity changes to structure, but not symmetrical structure, not the structure that reminds one of tedious marble halls, but a structure that has the mischievous sweat of a tricky world.

> I must tell you
> this young tree
> whose round and firm trunk
> between the wet
>
> pavement and the gutter
> (where water
> is trickling) rises
> bodily[13]

13. "Young Sycamore," lines 1-8. The whole poem was read. Complete text is in *CEP*, p. 332.

This is the music of biology. Very often what Williams does is, he takes something which is vegetative and compares it to something mechanical. Here it is the "round and firm trunk" and the "wet pavement and the gutter." Then it "rises bodily," and there is a lot of thrust in that word "bodily."

> it thins
> till nothing is left of it
> but two
>
> eccentric knotted
> twigs
> bending forward
> hornlike at the top[14]

There's a rising, taking care of the accurate procedures and mischief of biology (or, I should say, botany) with music. It represents what Williams wants in his own poems: the organic changed into accuracy, not leaving out anything; getting symmetry while welcoming chaos.

As I say that one of the things Williams gets into his poetry is the feeling of heaviness and lightness, the changing of a massive thing into something like thistledown—I must say that this can be got in rhyme too. I have talked of the *St. Louis Blues.* In terms of technique, we have lightness and heaviness in, say, one of the triplets of that blues:

Feelin' tomorrow the way I feel today,
Feelin' tomorrow the way I feel today,
Gonna pack my trunks and make my getaway.

14. Lines 18-24.

I happen to like "Young Sycamore" very much, but—do me something—I like that too.

A poem that has taken me (and I confess I first saw it in the French—it was translated by Eugène Jolas) is called "Portrait of the Author." I've come to see that Williams is a good representative of the possibilities of humanity. I believe that there is a certain simplicity, a desire to be straight in perception, honest in the best sense of the word, which I have seen as pretty charming. I look on most literary people as going too much for the gumshoe; as being devious in ambitious murk.

In this poem, we have a desire to be fair to every human being, a desire to see everything justly from within, a desire not to sum up, a desire not to go by the proclamations of the moment; a desire, in other words, to see, even where that seeing may be uncomfortable. That is a noble thing, and it is very hard to stick to.

In "Portrait of the Author," we have a presentation of an intense person who, while welcoming sometimes the almost unbearable things of the world, is trying to be just. It is a very good poem. It appeared first in *Sour Grapes* (so this book says).

The birches are mad with green points
the wood's edge is burning with their green,
burning, seething—No, no, no.

. . . .

Take me in your arms, tell me the commonest
thing that is in your mind to say,

say anything. I will understand you—!
It is the madness of the birch leaves opening
cold, one by one.[15]

In Williams' poems there is another presentation
of the relation of fury to quiet. In "Postlude," a very
popular poem, anthologized tremendously, the relation of intensity—great intensity—to quiet is presented.
In many poems, the two are presented. It is a big
thing in Williams' work, and it is a big thing, apparently, in his thoughts.

In the *Autobiography* there is a story of how Williams as a boy was chased by many boys, and he had
a wonderful time evading them, he just ran and
ran! Then he says: I either must run, or I must be
entirely still. Does that have something to do with
the technique of the line? Is a line still and very much
in motion? Yes. If one studies the syllables, the vowels,
one will see that. It arises from a big desire on the
part of persons to see the world entirely.

In a statement from *A Voyage to Pagany,* we have
the relation of fury to tranquillity. I have defined
happiness in one of the Aesthetic Realism writings as a
state of dynamic tranquillity. It could be called also
a state of tranquil mobility, or dynamism (but I want
to avoid using that word *dynamism*—it's been used by
the wrong people). In *A Voyage to Pagany* there is a
lot of intensity. There are some works that Williams
had to write because—well, it's almost like "Pike's

15. "Portrait of the Author," lines 1-3, 28-32. The whole poem
was read. Complete text is in *CEP*, pp. 228-229. See Williams'
comment following lecture, p. 105, and Siegel's letter, p. 29.

Peak or bust." In the chapter of *A Voyage to Pagany* called "Carcassonne," there is this passage:

> Why not just kill yourself. It's more sensible. And yet, he dreamed to go, madly, as he remembered at twelve he had sometimes done, madly, with no end in view; that day the kids couldn't catch him at hare and hounds, that phenomenally successful day when he had kept them baffled all the afternoon in a certain neighborhood, running, hiding, showing himself, doubling on his tracks, escaping, running again, showing himself and so on, hour after hour, running on. So, desperately scattered, he had remained *still;* whereas they, Jack and the rest, being always collected, could go loose. But if he should go loose, he would die, of this he was convinced, since to go loose to him was to go totally ungoverned.[16]

So there's a big desire for the quietness of crystal and the fury that one associates with a bacchic festival.

This has been a problem from the very beginning, and it is a major thing, because the world is a problem in rest and motion. There is nothing speedier than the world is; there is nothing quieter. Space is so quiet that no one can imagine how quiet it is—some space is; but even in that quiet, one can see much motion. You can just fill that space with madly innumerable crisscrossing lines.

This matter is very much in Williams' verse; and the relation also of heaviness and lightness is very

16. *A Voyage to Pagany* (New York: The Macaulay Company, 1928), p. 70.

much around. Sometimes it occurs in places where you wouldn't expect it. One place where you wouldn't expect it is in an essay on Aaron Burr, but I have to take books as I find them. There is a comparison between Washington and Burr. Apparently Williams liked Burr a little more. Well, I can't go into that.

> In fairness to them both, if there was ever an antithesis between two men, both good in essence, it was here, both fine but one the earth itself, the other—air. Somehow they should have joined.[17]

Does that say that earth and air should join? Should they join also in a line of poetry? Should there be space and obstruction? A management of space and obstruction is one of the things in the technique of a line. And Burr apparently here stands for space, and Washington for obstruction. I think that's the first time Washington and Burr have been used as to the nature of poetry. And I'm not being fanciful, the matter comes up in all kinds of ways.

Before I go on, I want to show that Williams as a doctor has also been concerned with the nature of poetry, the nature of art. There is a story about how Dr. Williams visited some of the distressed people (and he's done a lot of that) in the section of the stories, "Beer and Cold Cuts," and the story is called "Comedy Entombed: 1930." In this book there is a great restraint. The style is very different from the style of *In the American Grain,* very different from that in *A Voyage to Pagany.* It's a little bit like the

17. *In the American Grain* (New York: Albert & Charles Boni, 1925), p. 198.

style that Stendhal wanted to write, when he said, "I'm going to study the French Civil Code—not a bit of sentiment, nothing of myself, I'll give them just the facts." And the worship, in a sense, of the fact is something that we find in Williams' work. There is the phrase "no ideas but in things" or "no ideas but in the facts," which is very often quoted.

But getting to this passage:

> I have seldom seen such disorder and broken-ness—such a mass of unrelated parts of things lying about. That's it! I concluded to myself. An un-recognizable order! Actually—the new! And so good-natured and calm. So definitely the thing! And so compact. Excellent. And with such patina of use. Everything definitely "painty." Even the table, that way, pushed off from the center of the room.[18]

There's a desire to see the oneness of order and disorder, which is one of the big things: the relation of chaos to good sense. And in Williams' work from the very beginning, there is a pushing further of the meaning of chaos, and then the trying to see whether that belongs likewise to cause and effect or to order.

And we also find the relation of music to the visual effect. This is the big thing in poetry. Poetry goes after stillness and motion, and therefore goes after the visual and the musical. But that's a long story. Any-way, very often the visual becomes musical, and the other way round, in Williams' work. And we find that happening in places where we wouldn't expect it.

18. "Comedy Entombed: 1930," *Make Light of It*, p. 327.

Sometimes Williams honors light, sometimes he honors
sounds. I am going to read from *Make Light of It*
some passages in which he honors lights. This is a
very good sentence. I wish I had the time to go into
it. There is a drama here of lights and motion. It's
from a story called "The Dawn of Another Day." And
I must say this: that if it were put into lines, it would
be a poem. Jeremy Bentham gave a definition of
prose; he said: Prose is that kind of writing which goes
to the very end of the page and then comes back;
poetry is the kind that doesn't. It was a very useful
definition. Well, this goes to the end of the page and
comes back, but I can imagine that it might not.

> As it had already begun to grow dark you could
> see the first lights of the cars going back and forth
> intermittently beyond the two or three broken
> down houses on that shore, old houses occupied
> by Negroes, in whose windows also dim lights
> appeared.[19]

It's the relation of the lights of the cars and the
lights in the houses of the Negroes that has a possibility of poetry, and with a little change, it could be
poetry.

And there are effects of sounds in many ways.
Occasionally the American language, as it occurs in
most of the states of the union—very often in filling
stations, hamburger joints, et cetera—also occurs in
doctors' visits. This language has to do with poetry.
There are many samples, and my problem is to make
a good choice. This is from a story called "Country

19. "The Dawn of Another Day," *Make Light of It*, pp. 144-145.

Rain." It's about two women who are living together, and they have a little business. And they seem to be pretty satisfied, particularly Ruth.

> Everyone laughed immediately after he or she had said anything loud enough for all to hear, that was the custom.

This thinking that if you say something loud, you have to laugh—that is something.
Then we have also this:

> We missed you this morning.
> Ruth looked at them. Who do you think was making the pancakes?[20]

The way that is said takes some of the music of the world right into the customary lingo near the Atlantic and inland from the Atlantic.

Dr. Williams also is interested in silence and sound; he has a story which is really about that. There are certain people that occasionally Williams writes about with—well, more approbation than is customary. This is a story about a person who is on a Coast Guard cutter, or some official ship, cruising along the Aleutian Islands. The Americans meet some Russians, and they're going to have a good time. They're going to have a good time by breaking glasses.

> Everybody was high. Then they all stood up. We stood up too. A toast to the Czar! Down the brook. Then smash! They all whammed their

20. "Country Rain," *Make Light of It*, p. 309.

WILLIAMS' POETRY TALKED ABOUT 63

glasses on the floor. We looked at each other, then, wham! we followed suit. You couldn't ever use that glass for any other purpose again. The flunkeys came right in and started to sweep up.

So what did our Captain do but propose a toast to the President of the United States. Then wham! We smashed another lot of glasses on the floor. Boy! what a time we had singing and toasting each other with that beautiful glassware. What guys![21]

But that's joy! That's joy! That's why I object to Miss Koch's book, there's not enough joy in it. For joy of a certain kind there are places called "joy places," but when joy has the love of truth in it, as they used to say, the love of God in it—that's something else.

And then there's the joy of the Fourth of July. There is an interesting incident about this ship shooting off a cannon, and then all the people flee to the hills. This has a good relation of sound and quiet:

We only used a little one-pounder but you could hear each shot echoing way off into those hills, one shot following the other until it made quite a satisfying sort of a rumpus up there in that desolate silence.[22]

Many of Williams' poems could be called "Quite a Satisfying Sort of a Rumpus"; and I'd like more rumpus.

There are many examples of this kind of language. There is a using of the rhythms of speech in a very taking way. An example is:

21. "In Northern Waters," *Make Light of It,* pp. 262-263.
22. *Make Light of It,* p. 263.

He doesn't look so good but he likes it here.[23]

That has cadence. There are many other samples.

However, jumping back now, I'm going to read a poem which I think is very good, and from what I learned from Miss Koch it seems that Williams himself likes it a good deal. He should. Sometimes an author is right. And it has been much discussed. Apparently it was discussed by Yvor Winters—R. P. Blackmur or Yvor Winters. Well, what those gentlemen do before they get through with a poem—you'd think that the poem existed to be discussed.

This is a poem which tries to get together two things. There is a great deal to do with what happens to the body. The use of the word *contagious* here is a bringing out of new possibility. *Contagious* essentially means spreading from one place to another; it's come to take on a rather terrible meaning. There is a trip to the contagious hospital while spring is having a difficult time. But it's going to get there—it usually does. This is called "Spring and All." I have looked at this poem very carefully, and it stands up very well.

> By the road to the contagious hospital
> under the surge of the blue
> mottled clouds driven from the
> northeast—a cold wind. Beyond, the
> waste of broad, muddy fields
> brown with dried weeds, standing and fallen[24]

23. "Verbal Transcription—6 A.M.," *Make Light of It*, p. 285.
24. Lines 1-6. The whole poem was read. Text is in *CEP*, pp. 241-242.

This is a making of even the growing of twigs, bushes, leaves, a mighty sad but still interesting procedure. It would be interesting to compare these lines:

> They enter the new world naked,
> cold, uncertain of all
> save that they enter[25]

with some of the abnegatory lines of Eliot. He's always entering into the world in a rather sad form, while getting out of it in a sad form. And he's always penitent. Penitence is very popular. I wonder why? Maybe there's something to be penitent about.

But anyway, the sadness that is here is a lively sadness, while the sadness that one sees in "Ash Wednesday" is the sadness that has in it a too self-pleased smirk. There is a great deal of the smirk in present-day verse. The smirk is hidden, but it's there.

This is not the time to go lengthily into the technique of "Spring and All," but I believe that it is important to see that an effect which is similar can be had in another way. The lines I'm referring to are from Coleridge's *Christabel*. Now Coleridge's *Christabel* is honest rhyming; it's very beautiful. I am pleased by the music in Williams' work, I am pleased by *Christabel*. There is more similarity than difference, because there is honest music. There is more similarity between a quatrain that is honestly musical and honest free verse than there is between honest free verse and not so honest free verse. So these are the lines from *Christabel*:

25. "Spring and All," lines 16-18.

> There is not wind enough to twirl
> The one red leaf, the last of its clan,
> That dances as often as dance it can,
> Hanging so light, and hanging so high,
> On the topmost twig that looks up at the sky.

Coleridge influenced Yeats, and Yeats has influenced ever so many people.

As we go on with the consideration of work, the thing that I'd like to say is that in finding Williams' work good, I have used all the classical and non-classical and semi-classical, romantic and semi-romantic and demi-romantic and quasi-romantic and pseudo-romantic perhaps—all the statements of the critics. And what it seems Williams should feel is that the value of his work arises from the fact that he has added one new way of seeing the world, that arose from him, that without him wouldn't be; that where this is honest, it goes along with honesty anywhere else; and that the honesty is something that makes work seemingly different, similar.

In order to show this, I am going to read for a while from a work which Dr. Williams himself apparently has spurned. He hasn't included it in his reprinted work. I like it very much. I think that there is a continuity between what is said in *Kora in Hell* and what is said even in *Paterson*. There is a trying to see. The best thing about Williams is that he's not given up seeing; and he talks of "one day" and "one night" because he wants to give that unspoiled unity and freshness to it.

This is from *Kora in Hell,* apparently written in

1917 but published by the Four Seas Company in 1920; and as far as I know, this is the only edition now extant:

> The true value is that peculiarity which gives an object a character by itself. The associational or sentimental value is the false.[26]

This has to do with imagism, partly; but the statement made in Victorian times, "Have your eye on the object," goes along with it. And the desire to be exact that we see in the *Greek Anthology* occasionally, goes along with it. No artist has ever been unfair to the object. Sometimes it is necessary to say, "Brothers, we are becoming unfair to the object," but no artist as artist has ever *been* unfair; and *how* people are fair to the object—that is a big thing.

Let's take another statement:

> The imagination goes from one thing to another. Given many things of nearly totally divergent natures but possessing one-thousandth part of a quality in common, provided that be new, distinguished, these things belong in an imaginative category and not in a gross natural array.[27]

I once discussed Leigh Hunt's "What Is Poetry?" Leigh Hunt happens to have written some good poetry, and in this essay he says, among other things, that

26. Prologue, *Kora in Hell: Improvisations* (Boston: The Four Seas Company, 1920), p. 16. Since the lecture was given, a new edition was published by City Lights Books (1957). The City Lights edition does not include the Prologue.

27. Prologue, *Kora*, p. 16.

poetry has to have variety and unity, unity and variety. This is what Williams is saying, really. It is true. It is a revivification of the idea, even of *e pluribus unum*— from many, one. It simply means that there should be teamwork among words and perceptions, intense teamwork. Art can be considered as being intense teamwork: teamwork that you don't expect, but still teamwork.

George Saintsbury, whom I see as one of the joyous and one of the greatest critics, also one of the greatest writers who has ever lived, said in the preface to *Seventeenth-Century Lyrics* (among many places) something about manyness and oneness; but then he also said: Deal with the common as if it were uncommon, that's one of the things in poetry. That goes along with Williams' idea of taking the tawdry, the unimportant, the slatternly, and showing that there is the wonderful in it.

What Williams has done in New Jersey is to show another possibility of what Saintsbury said in a rather academic way—though he isn't very academic, really: he also jumps around a good deal; he's a great user of the parenthesis. And I was interested in seeing in one of the issues of *The Dial* that there was a review by George Saintsbury in over his eightieth year; and right after it, Williams is reviewing *Good Morning, America* by Carl Sandburg, not being able to make up his mind about it, apparently: he says good and bad things of it. But they follow each other, Saintsbury and Williams, and I said, What have we here? I know something of what Saintsbury has looked for because a person looks for these things in poetry: music become sight, the words placed in such a way that the world comes into a delightful flame.

Kora is a statement of Williams' way of looking at the world which as I see it should not be superseded. The style of writing has changed, the line sometimes seems different in *Paterson* from the early work, but whatever is in that early work is as fresh—more fresh —than next week's issue of *Time*. Every artist has a difficulty about choosing the means of representing himself best; but there are certain effects in that early work that should be looked on as tomorrow-ish.

There is a Prologue to *Kora in Hell*, which is critical. In that prologue, by the way, Williams says that Eliot is doing a rehash of Baudelaire and Rimbaud and God knows what all. And he repeats that in his autobiography. It seems that Williams has tried to be polite; I believe that with Eliot, one shouldn't be so poignant. There is a passage in the *Autobiography* about Eliot, and it sounds like the statement made to Joe Jackson: "Say it isn't true, Joe."

> These were the years just before the great catastrophe to our letters—the appearance of T. S. Eliot's *The Waste Land*. There was heat in us, a core and a drive that was gathering headway and upon the theme of a rediscovery of a primary impetus, the elementary principle of all art, in the local conditions.[28]

All art is both local and universal. Sometimes it goes from the universal and gets to the local. There is a line

28. *Autobiography*, p. 146.

from Dante's *Paradiso* that Eliot quotes which is not local: "*e la sua volontate è nostra pace.*" It's a very beautiful line. "And his will is our peace." It doesn't have twigs in it, but it's a good line.

> Our work staggered to a halt for a moment under the blast of Eliot's genius which gave the poem back to the academics. We did not know how to answer him.[29]

That was good seeing. Eliot is academic. Even though he seems to be the leader of the latest thing, he is academic.

There is this distress about the academic in *Kora in Hell*, too. I regard this work as very important. I think it should be lectured on in colleges: the meaning of it.

In *Kora in Hell* there are a few things that sound very corybantic. I can't imagine Eliot dancing, but I'd like to see him. There is very much about the dance in *Kora in Hell*. I talked about the dance lately and showed its relation to all art: how the body becomes light through it; and I was taken by these passages:

> Thus a poem is tough . . . solely from that attenuated power which draws perhaps many broken things into a dance giving them thus a full being.[30]

This accents lightness: out of weight comes lightness, out of confusion comes symmetry. But the word *dance* is used.

Then in the best sense of the word, there is what

29. *Autobiography*, p. 146.
30. Prologue, *Kora*, p. 19.

can be called the democracy of imagination. It seems that Williams has listened to people humbly; he has watched housewives and listened to them, and he has learned. Very few people want to do that. And though there is in this book a great discontent, there is a desire to be fair which is decidedly taking. We have passages like the following:

> Those who permit their senses to be despoiled of the things under their noses by stories of all manner of things removed and unattainable are of frail imagination. . . . A frail imagination, unequal to the tasks before it, is easily led astray.[31]

The word *imagination* is used a great deal, and I take it to mean the desire to be fair to an object, both in itself and in what it has to do with other objects, no matter how far it can get.

Then there are words about composition:

> It is only the music of the instruments which is joined and that not by the woodworker but by the composer, by virtue of the imagination.
> On this level of the imagination all things and ages meet in fellowship.[32]

This means that if I say that Williams' work is related to something maybe honest in the Byzantine, he shouldn't mind, because somewhere the honesty that is in New Jersey goes along with the honesty in Byzantium.

31. Prologue, *Kora*, p. 21.
32. Prologue, *Kora*, p. 21.

On this level of the imagination all things and ages meet in fellowship. Thus only can they, peculiar and perfect, find their release. This is the beneficent power of the imagination.[33]

(The word *beneficent* wouldn't be used now. It would be looked on as too "soft." It would be said that this is the "corrosive" power of the imagination.)

A further passage. There is a lot about flowering. The word *flowering* has always meant something good, as we see in the word *flourish*. When things prosper, they flourish, and that comes from the word *flower*. There is a strange arrangement—Williams says he got it from the Italian eighteenth-century poet and musician, Metastasio—it's got codas, and sections. (Pound was very fond of codas.) I may say that there is a coda, as far as I remember, in *Paterson*, too. Well, a coda is a statement that is at the end of something and, though it is apart, tends to help sum it up or add to it. It is the same word as *tail*, really. I have always been puzzled by the word, though.

A poet witnessing the chicory flower and realizing its virtues of form and color so constructs his praise of it as to borrow no particle from right or left. He gives his poem over to the flower and its plant themselves that they may benefit by those cooling winds of the imagination which thus returned upon them will refresh them at their task of saving the world.[34]

This is very much related to Aesthetic Realism, because aesthetics, according to Aesthetic Realism, is the

33. Prologue, *Kora,* p. 21.   34. Prologue, *Kora,* p. 22.

highest kind of honesty. Williams here says that if the "cooling winds of the imagination" return upon the flower and its plant, they "will refresh them at their task of saving the world." "Saving the world" suddenly! This is what I meant when I said that the honesty that is in Williams' poems has got some notion of a world also coming into form. The idea appeared early. And the desire of getting the world into form is the big thing that we see in the tackling of all the confusion, past and present, in *Paterson.*

Then there is a statement quoted from Kandinsky about what every artist has to do. This is almost in tabular form:

> Every artist has to express himself.
> Every artist has to express his epoch.
> Every artist has to express the pure and eternal qualities of the art of all men.[35]

That is what I mean by the democracy of the imagination. But there is distinction, too.

So far, these quotations have been from the *Kora in Hell* Prologue, which is critical. Then there is prose which can be considered as a little bit like that of the West Wind, if it were writing. There is a lot of dancing around, but it's good. There is some writing which goes dancing around hither and thither, up and down, and there is more dynamics than accuracy; here I think there is dynamics and also accuracy. But I can see where this would be a little frowned on by the persons who want verse to be like thuds on carpet. This is from Section 3 of Part II of the Improvisations:

35. Prologue, *Kora*, p. 27.

Hark! it is the music! Whence does it come? What! Out of the ground? Is it this that you have been preparing for me? Ha, goodbye, I have a rendez vous in the tips of three birch sisters. *Encouragé vos musiciens!* Ask them to play faster. I will return—later. Ah you are kind.—and I? must dance with the wind, make my own snow flakes, whistle a contrapuntal melody to my own fuge! Huzza then, this is the dance of the blue moss bank! Huzza then, this is the mazurka of the hollow log! Huzza then, this is the dance of rain in the cold trees.[36]

That dance of the blue moss bank should remain! There's no reason not to have it! And the interesting thing is that word *dance* related to moss.

Then there is a passage which is related to the Coleridge line about the one leaf:

So far away August green as it yet is. They say the sun still comes up o'mornings and it's harvest moon now. Always one leaf at the peak twig swirling, swirling and apples rotting in the ditch.[37]

Here again we have the desire to put together motion and rest. The apples rotting in the ditch are one kind of motion, and the swirling leaf is something else.

Then we have writing that can be seen as a little bit like Rimbaud. There is something you begin with, and then you have a swift associative jump—which sometimes is too swift for the reader. But the question is, is it honest? As I see it, these jumps are honest.

36. *Kora*, p. 36. City Lights ed., p. 13.
37. *Kora*, p. 37. City Lights ed., p. 14.

What can it mean to you that a child wears pretty clothes and speaks three languages or that its mother goes to the best shops? It means: July has good need of his blazing sun. But if you pick one berry from the ash tree I'd not know it again for the same no matter how the rain washed. Make my bed of witchhazel twigs, said the old man, since they bloom on the brink of winter.[38]

There is a rhythm to the prose. There is a different rhythm in *Make Light of It*.

Talking about rhythm, there is another matter: the relation of the rhythm of prose to the rhythm of the line. Saintsbury is one of the persons who has written on that subject: *The History of English Prose Rhythm.* I don't believe that he's said even the penultimate word, but the fact is, he has taken prose rhythm very seriously, and he has shown that there is a relation of heavy and light syllables.

Going on with the idea of the democracy of imagination, Williams, though seeing himself as a poet, says that even in commercial people there is a desire for art. And that is said so seldom. Most often, we just want to *épater la bourgeoisie,* we want to shock them into abasement. They can do it themselves—we don't have to try.

Living with and upon and among the poor, those that gather in a few rooms, sometimes very clean, sometimes full of vermine, there are certain pestilential individuals, priests, school teachers, doctors, commercial agents of one sort or another who

38. *Kora*, p. 37. City Lights ed., pp. 14-15.

though they themselves are full of graceful perfections nevertheless contrive to be so complacent of their lot, floating as they are with the depth of a sea beneath them, as to be worthy only of amused contempt. Yet even to these sometimes there rises that which they think in their ignorance is a confused babble of aspiring voices not knowing what ancient harmonies these are to which they are so faultily listening.[39]

That is very humane: the idea of a vice-president of a bank having harmonies in him.

The matter of fake and honesty has been put by Williams in ever so many ways. Sometimes he wondered, maybe if he was somewhat more adroit, he'd get further: look what all these people are doing. Here he makes it a fight between the lamps and the sun. It is well said:

Throw that flower in the waste basket, it's faded. And keep an eye to your shoes and fingernails. The fool you once laughed at has made a fortune! There's small help in a clutter of leaves either, no matter how they gleam. Punctillio's the thing. A nobby vest. Spats. Lamps carry far, believe me, in lieu of sunshine![40]

That is well said, and I don't see why it should be disregarded. I think if that were put in verse form, what would happen to it is what could happen, let us say, to Lincoln's Gettysburg Address—there's rhythm there.

The next thing has to do with technique. I have said that a line is a glide and a jump. Also I have men-

39. *Kora*, p. 47. City Lights ed., p. 26.
40. *Kora*, p. 51. City Lights ed., p. 31.

tioned that Williams at times has the motion of a pickaninny in his verse, and he talks about how a pickaninny runs. This is interesting:

Desire skates like a Hollander as well as runs pickaninny fashion.[41]

Which means, that it jumps and it also glides.

The most beautiful thing about a line is that the two desires of man are satisfied in a line of poetry: activity and quietude. I talked in an Aesthetic Realism class of the life of Francis Parkman: he wanted to be among the Indians, but he had to be in his room, writing painfully. There was a tremendous desire to climb peaks, to go into the West, which he satisfied with *The Oregon Trail*; but we see in his life that there was a great desire also to be still. Those things which are in people are the things which words, all the time, are settling in their way. We have this beautifully put in the following sentence:

Violence has begotten peace, peace has fluttered away in agitation.[42]

Then there is the desire, which Williams has had, of participating very much in things—crawling, as it were, within the trunk of life—and then the being aloof from it. This is shown in this passage of Improvisations XII:

The trick is never to touch the world anywhere. Leave yourself at the door, walk in, admire the pic-

41. *Kora*, p. 53. City Lights ed., p. 35.
42. *Kora*, p. 56. City Lights ed., p. 39.

tures, talk a few words with the master of the house, question his wife a little, rejoin yourself at the door —and go off arm in arm listening to last week's symphony played by angel hornsmen from the benches of a turned cloud.[43]

Well, that is very nice.

And then we have this passage:

And imagining himself to be two persons he eases his mind by putting his burdens upon one while the other takes what pleasure there is before him.[44]

That means a great deal.

Another interesting thing in the line is, that lines should be high and low. There is a digging deep. And very often in Williams' writings there is a feeling that if you dig, you will get to space and freedom. I could show this in one way or another in many poems in both volumes of the collected poems. Sometimes it's not so obvious, but here we have it pretty straight. I should say that Williams, trying to be friendly, sometimes says "mon cher," "mon ami," "townspeople," "my friends," and that is very taking. Here we have "mon ami":

Dig deeper *mon ami*, the rock maidens are running naked in the dark cellars.[45]

And what I have seen as an understanding of mothers is in a passage here. It is an aesthetic problem,

43. *Kora*, p. 56. City Lights ed., p. 39.
44. *Kora*, p. 56. City Lights ed., p. 40.
45. *Kora*, p. 58. City Lights ed., p. 42.

how a person should see his mother. Williams has been
very much affected by that. In the *Later Poems*, there
is a poem about a mother's last days. It has a dream
which interested me a great deal, about a tiger who
was both fierce and, it seems, looking for a rest. It is
called "Two Pendants" and it is a very good thing. In
another poem, "Eve," and in quite a few other places,
there is a desire to see a mother both kindly and critically. Some of the most honest writing about mothers,
I have seen in Williams' works. But we see the beginning of that in a passage from *Kora in Hell*. (I should
say that Kora means Persephone, who lived above
ground half the year and below half the year.) Well,
this is about the mother:

> A woman on the verge of growing old kindles in the
> mind of her son a certain curiosity which spinning
> upon itself catches the woman herself in its wheel,
> stripping from her the accumulations of many harsh
> years and shows her at last full of an old time sup-
> pleness hardly to have been guessed by the stiffened
> exterior which had held her fast till that time.[46]

In Williams' early work there is talk about the four-
teen-year-old who is too jaunty and doesn't want to
see people of all ages. That is good, because you're
never too young to understand, or try to understand.

A further passage is on how a poem is made. Now,
a poem is made casually and deliberately, in varying
degrees (the casual would stand for the spontaneous).
It is the making one which we see in a river. Williams
is very much given to the river. The river is that which

46. *Kora*, pp. 66-67. City Lights ed., p. 54.

moves as it remains. In an early work, Williams insults the Passaic; he does so in *In the American Grain*—he calls it the swillhouse. Later, it seems, he was kinder to the Passaic.

A river is something which is because it moves. A line should be like that. And some of the going sideways while sticking to a point, is in this passage:

That which is heard from the lips of those to whom we are talking in our day's-affairs mingles with what we see in the streets and everywhere about us as it mingles also with our imaginations.[47]

There is a kind of chemistry. We see things, and they become us. Williams' works are one of the best examples of the meaning in Whitman's poem, "There Was a Child Went Forth."

A statement which Miss Koch quotes is interesting because—well, its meaning is just illimitable:

After thirty years of staring at one true phrase he discovered that its opposite was true also.[48]

There is a dealing with lies, and the constant thing is: How can there be the sun, and a moon, and a flower—a begonia, or chicory, or anemone—and still all these lies? How can the world be this way?

It's lies, walking, spitting, breathing, coughing lies that bloom, shine sun, shine moon.[49]

47. *Kora*, p. 63. City Lights ed., p. 49.
48. *Kora,* p. 68. City Lights ed., p. 57.
49. *Kora,* p. 72. City Lights ed., p. 62.

That is a prelude to *Paterson:* about how the world can seem to be going on unspoiled while there is all this dishonest junk.

Then there is a relation between light and dark:

> That which is known has value only by virtue of the dark. This cannot be otherwise. A thing known passes out of the mind into the muscles, the will is quit of it, save only when set into vibration by the forces of darkness opposed to it.[50]

That is physiology, but it is also criticism. What happens when a thought comes into us? What happens even physiologically? That could be commented on very much.

A further passage is about how all objects can make for wonder:

> The particular thing, whether it be four pinches of four divers white powders cleverly compounded to cure surely, safely, pleasantly a painful twitching of the eyelids or say a pencil sharpened at one end, dwarfs the imagination, makes logic a butterfly, offers a finality that sends us spinning through space, a fixity the mind could climb forever, a revolving mountain, a complexity with a surface of glass: the gist of poetry.[51]

Williams is constantly trying to change flatness into relief and motion. He does that in a poem called "The Term" which deals with paper that gets rumpled, and then flat—but it stays, I think, rumpled.

50. *Kora,* p. 77. City Lights ed., p. 71.
51. *Kora,* p. 85. City Lights ed., p. 82.

Then there is a passage about the one day. In *Paterson*, something that is now quoted and has come to be decidedly known, is the passage about one night; but there is a prelude to that in the one day of *Kora in Hell*:

Seeing the leaves dropping from the high and low branches the thought rises: this day of all others is the one chosen, all other days fall away from it on either side and only itself remains in perfect fulness.[52]

That is in relation to this bit of music from *Paterson* about the one night. And since I want to deal with early work and late work, I'm going to read this passage. It is lyrical; it is suffused with the mysterious lusciousness of night.

On this most voluptuous night of the year
the term of the moon is yellow with no light

. . . .
Now love might enjoy its play
and nothing disturb the full octave of its run.[53]

Here love is presented as a rich tranquillity that doesn't have to be taken back; and there is a good deal in Williams' writings of love that has to be taken back.

So we find that some things in *Paterson* could very well be in the *Kora in Hell*. Take a statement like this, about virtue:

52. *Kora*, p. 85. City Lights ed., p. 83.
53. *Paterson*, p. 105. The whole passage was read.

> Virtue,
> my kitten, is a complex reward in all
> languages, achieved slowly.[54]

There is much ethics there.

And the notion of language in *Paterson* is really coherent with what is said in *Kora in Hell*:

> So much talk of the language—when there are no
> ears
>
> . . . .
>
> But it is true, they fear
> it more than death, beauty is feared
> more than death, more than they fear death
>
> Beautiful thing
>
> —and marry only to destroy, in private, in
> their privacy only to destroy, to hide[55]

That means very much. As they say in the French, beaucoup and toujours.

Then the business about the dance is put in another way. It seems that Williams once saw a tin roof rising. I imagine he saw it, because it seems everything he writes about, he saw. This does give a feeling: it's the first time, as far as I know, that verse has been made of a tin roof flying.

> a shriek of fire with
> the upwind, whirling the room away—to reveal

54. *Paterson*, p. 220.

55. *Paterson*, p. 129. The passage quoted was from "So much talk of the language" through "not infamy, not death."

the awesome sight of a tin roof (1880)
entire, half a block long, lifted like a
skirt, held by the fire—to rise at last,
almost with a sigh, rise and float, float
upon the flames as upon a sweet breeze,
and majestically drift off, riding the air[56]

We have statements about the poem, and though
Williams says again and again that the poem should
be local, again and again he says it's also about the
whole world—which, of course, it is. You have to be
somewhere before you can be anywhere.

The province of the poem is the world.
When the sun rises, it rises in the poem
and when it sets darkness comes down
and the poem is dark   .[57]

There is much about dark and light; and there is a
passage about genius and syllables. Sometimes Williams seems to think that poetry is so hard to get, it's
a matter really of centuries. Sometimes he thinks he
picks it up in every place he visits.

—in a hundred years, perhaps—
the syllables
                (with genius)

56. *Paterson*, p. 147. The passage quoted was from "a shriek of fire" through "(but not our minds)".
57. *Paterson*, p. 122. The passage quoted here was from "The province of the poem" through "in the dark."

                              or perhaps
        two lifetimes

        Sometimes it takes longer   .[58]

    Then Williams describes a relation, which has al-
ways been—it was among the troubadours—in every
person: the desire to see and the desire to love, and
the way the two can fight:

    Did I do more than share your guilt, sweet
        woman. The
    cherimoya is the most delicately flavored of all
    tropic fruit. . .   Either I abandon you
    or give up writing   .[59]

This question has been for a very long time.

    As I said, there is very much to say about this work.
I have talked lengthily on "The Red Wheelbarrow,"
which is an anthology piece now, but as Williams says
(he uses cuss words very often), that doesn't mean
a damn—it is still good, whether it's printed a hundred
times. Even if it got on television, it would still be
what it is. You can't spoil a thing simply because you
repeat it often. *Hamlet*, for example, has gone through
ever so many forms, but it's still as new as tomorrow's
plums.
    In "The Red Wheelbarrow" there is religion. There
is a mingling, in short, of qualities: visual, musical, in

58. *Paterson*, p. 171.
59. *Paterson*, p. 171.

a sense mystical. I think that Williams' poem is better, but I am going to read Tennyson's "Flower in the Crannied Wall" because the two poems have a similarity of purpose. This is very good, but it has some meretriciousness to it. The absence of the meretricious in the Williams poem is notable.—This is Tennyson:

> Flower in the crannied wall,
> I pluck you out of the crannies,
> I hold you here, root and all, in my hand,
> Little flower—but *if* I could understand
> What you are, root and all, and all in all,
> I should know what God and man is.

Instead of putting it in rhyme, Williams says, "So much depends." That way is better. Tennyson begins with the flower and says, "Look, I would know what the whole world means if I knew what this flower is!" What Williams says is, "So much depends on this red wheelbarrow." The direction is different, but the trip has a similarity.

This is a great poem. It can be anthologized, and people can get sick of hearing it (in quotes) and Williams himself can get sick of hearing about it—the fact remains. Williams uses a phrase "saw the god" in *A Voyage to Pagany*; well, here all the gods are seen. And so it is only right that "The Red Wheelbarrow" be read once more. This is seemingly one of the most innocent little poems; it's just creeping like a waif into a big mansion.

> so much depends
> upon[60]

60. The whole poem was read. Text is in *CEP*, p. 277.

The value of the world depends upon that red wheelbarrow. It is in keeping with Williams' other ideas, that if one thing can be seen straight, we shall come to a notion of a world truly of us. The technique, however, is what makes it; technique in the best sense. Technique I define generally as a way of dealing honestly with an object, so that the utmost impression can be had by the person then seeing it. And there are various ways of doing this. In other words, to bring out the power of an object is the purpose of technique.

Now, the syllables here are different. It is hard to say why "depends upon" falls differently from "a red wheelbarrow," but from one point of view, it is very easy. "N" is a grudging sound, "upon" is grudging; "red" and "wheel," particularly, are more round. One is grudging and the other is luscious. And then we have the relation of the visual to the form. A circle is usually seen as quite pallid. A circle is geometric. But giving it red takes the eternity of the circle (the circle does stand for eternity—it is represented in the old legends by the snake with its tail in its mouth) and gives it motion. Consequently, to say that there is red in this wheelbarrow, and also the feeling of solidity, brings together all the weight and lightness that Williams has been looking for in his work. And it is done very subtly. I could talk about this a great deal, including the meaning of the wheel, also the relation of the wheel to the other part of the barrow, and the fact that it is handled by a person.

"Glazed with rain"—here again we have the feeling of polish and roughness. Take silk. Silk is admirable because it shines; tweed can be admirable because it doesn't shine. There is a relation between polish and roughness. The red wheelbarrow, of course, is still a wheelbarrow; then it's glazed with rain—which means that the roughness of the world, the ordinariness of the world, has taken on a polish. It takes on a Veronese quality.

All this has motion in it, but the word "beside" is very still; and then "the white chickens," whether they're white or not, are still very much in motion: they flutter around like those sparrows.

So this whole poem is a study in what the nature of reality is. I'm not trying to be portentous. I remember a statement in the *New York Times Book Review* that Williams was very much taken with this poem, "The Red Wheelbarrow." I read it, and I felt he had a right to be, as I said in my review.

This is a major poem, but again it should be seen as related to other poems. It is related to the flower poem of Tennyson; it is related to a poem that now sounds so old-fashioned, of T. E. Brown. Brown himself was a Manxman and he went around with the rough people of the Isle of Man, but this sounds awfully sentimental, and it has been used by the gardeners sickeningly. However, I don't care how a poem has been used, I want to see the poem itself. I don't care whether it says "God wot" or "God knows." This poem is not as good as the Williams poem, and it is not as good as the Tennyson poem, but it is in the same field:

> A garden is a lovesome thing, God wot!
> Rose plot,
> Fringed pool,
> Fern'd grot—

The veriest school
Of peace; and yet the fool
Contends that God is not—
Not God! in gardens! when the eve is cool?
Nay, but I have a sign;
'Tis very sure God walks in mine.[61]

Well, God walked beside the white chickens—something like God.

I have to conclude shortly, but I am going to read what Mr. Keats would call in *Endymion* certain samples of the "joy forever."

This has suspense. It is a little bit like that music they used to use when the villain came in. It is called "Poem":

> as the cat
> climbed over
> the top of
>
> the jamcloset[62]

That is a poem of suspense!

Then there is a poem about a flower radiating and going everywhere. I can't read all of it, but this is very nice:

> One petal goes eight blocks
>
> past two churches and a brick school beyond

61. T. E. Brown, "My Garden."
62. The whole poem was read. Text is in *CEP*, p. 340.

the edge of the park where under trees

leafless now, women having nothing else to do
sit in summer—to the small house

in which I happen to have been born.[63]

There is a use, which can be overdone, of typographical effects. Cummings uses these effects, and I can't go for them: you're not going to make a poem by capitals or punctuation or even spaces. However, the following poem is very good. It gets in the collage effect, which painters use—that is, getting newspaper headlines and things in. (There is a business about horses in the *Voyage to Pagany:* about horses representing the beauty of the world too. There is a time when Dev Evans, who has a certain similarity to the writer, is going with Miss Black to the *Reitschüle* in Vienna, where they make horses do lovely things.) This is from "Rapid Transit":

THE HORSES   black
                        &
PRANCED   white

Outings in New York City

Ho for the open country

. . . .
Take the Pelham Bay Park Branch
of the Lexington Ave. (East Side)

63. "The Flower," lines 14-19. *CEP*, p. 236.

Line and you are there in a few
minutes

Interborough Rapid Transit Co.[64]

Then there is a lovely effect in a poem, "Fine Work
with Pitch and Copper," which I don't believe is as
good as "Rapid Transit" with its finality; but this gives
a prelude to the tough language when it's at its best
in the stories:

One still chewing
picks up a copper strip
and runs his eye along it[65]

This is also preluded in *Kora in Hell*, because it has
to do with the vertical and the horizontal. There is a
motion going up and down—the chewing—and then
there is the looking at the copper strip.

And there is a poem which is simple description (if
Zola loved poetry, he'd love this) called "The Sun
Bathers":

A tramp thawing out
on a doorstep
against an east wall
Nov. 1, 1933[66]

64. Lines 1-4, 13-17. The first seventeen lines of the poem
were read. Text is in *CEP*, p. 282.
65. "Fine Work with Pitch and Copper," lines 16-18. *CEP*,
p. 368.
66. Lines 1-4. The whole poem was read. Text is in *CEP*,
p. 457.

That is straight stuff.

And there is the "Two Pendants"; as I said, I wish I could read that.

But I am going to close with a poem—it is a good poem—which is autobiographic (it has a right to be); and it is the poet defiant. The word *cure* can have various meanings: we can be cured of heartache, we can be cured of financial ills, we can be cured of anything that is inaccurate.—Occasionally, Williams has been too humble. I think he was too humble as to Eliot—well, many people were. And there was this feeling of Williams that there was something going on in himself which didn't seem to be in the Eliot field, even in that of Edwin Arlington Robinson. Many people were very much impressed by him, but there is more poetry in that "Red Wheelbarrow" than in all of Robinson's *Tristram*.

This is a poem which is definitely autobiographic; it is called "The Cure":

> Sometimes I envy others, fear them
> a little too, if they write well.
>
> . . . .
> But they have no access to my sources.
>
> . . . .
> where we walk daily and from which
> among the rest you have sprung
> and opened flower-like to my hand.[67]

It is a true poem. Williams says that he is honoring earth, including the earth of New Jersey and the earth

67. Lines 1-2, 5, 10-12. The whole poem was read. Text is in *Collected Later Poems*, p. 23.

of all time, and that somehow earth feels honored in him, and that occasionally there is petulance and uncertainty (as there's been, I'm sure, a lot of). But out of it all have come two things: at the moment there is a great deal of fame, and I hope that Dr. Williams enjoys it; but most of all, the fame is deserved. And the poetry has helped the America that he has wanted so much to care for.

EDITORS' NOTE. *William Carlos Williams rose, shook Eli Siegel's hand, and said: "I am astonished. I value your words." Then he sat down again and continued.*

WILLIAMS. I can see your direction through it, and it's very important.

SIEGEL. Well, I think poetry should make one happy.

WILLIAMS. Well, it seems that the poetry that has been written in the past only leads you to something else that you want to do. When you're restless, and you don't know where you're going, you feel distressed, that's all. Practically, I feel more distress than happiness, and as far as the fame is concerned—well, I got left out of the anthology of Mr. Oscar Williams.

SIEGEL. No, there's one you're in. And that's a questionable Oscar anyway.

WILLIAMS. Yes.

SIEGEL. I know you're in the *New Poems*, with a photograph.

SHELDON KRANZ. "The Yachts" is in that one.

SIEGEL. About that poem, I disagree with some of the critics; it doesn't go along with your customary joy.

WILLIAMS. Well, that's something that stands apart—I mean it's something that I never particularly enjoyed.

SIEGEL. It's in the Oxford anthology, Matthiessen uses it—

WILLIAMS. I think it's because it's more conventional.

SIEGEL. Maybe.

WILLIAMS. That's why they liked it. It was more or less of a stunt, although it came up at the end.

SIEGEL. It's got that tragedy in it.

WILLIAMS. Yeah, they liked that.

SIEGEL. I like things in *Kora in Hell* better.

WILLIAMS. Yes.—I don't know what to say, about your whole talk—certainly you're a rare person. It's just as important—it's as if everything I've ever done has been for you. You come up with it, and so few people come up with anything. They don't come up with it at all. They praise the wrong things, for the wrong reasons very often, although it seems plain enough; and when you say it, it's plain. You make it plain. And it's very forceful.

SIEGEL. What I'd like some time is a closer examination of certain passages—if you'd like—

WILLIAMS. Yes.

SIEGEL. I wish that could be.

WILLIAMS. It's wonderful, what you've covered. I never thought anybody had ever looked at the stuff like that. I never thought—

SIEGEL. I've got lots more. For instance, I wanted to discuss your review of Antheil—do you remember, that was in *Transition?*

WILLIAMS. Yes, yes. You mean about the concert in Carnegie Hall?

SIEGEL. Yes, there are certain statements in the *Transition* review. And then in the *Voyage to Pagany*

there are many things, particularly about your deal-
ings with the Venus and sculpture, and your feeling
about sculpture. I mentioned to Barbara Lekberg
that you had said in the *Autobiography* that wherever you see sculpture, you just wish it were the
original stone still, or something like that. But then,
in the *Voyage to Pagany* you have this great intensity.

WILLIAMS. That was referring to myself, as far as I was
concerned. I really did go through a stage when I
wanted to do something and I didn't know what I
wanted to do, and I considered sculpture. But it
wasn't for me, that was all.

SIEGEL. Do you want to hear that passage?

WILLIAMS. Sure. I guess.

SIEGEL. It's a good passage.

WILLIAMS. Yeah? All right.

SIEGEL. It's very good. In fact, the parts about your
reaction to those things in Rome and Naples—

WILLIAMS. Oh, I can remember one of the statues at
Rome, but that wasn't my feeling toward sculpture,
it was my feeling toward Venus.

SIEGEL. It doesn't sound just like that. There's a changing from stone to Venus. Well, anyway:

Rome starting alive from the rock. He felt it, he
could touch the fragments. There IS the Venus.
There it *is*. Where? There, crouching at the top of
the stairs. But that is a stone. No, it is Venus! It is
she. No, it is a stone. It is she, I say. Venus! The
presence is over the stone.
   Evans was near mad with it. He felt himself pos-
sessed, bewitched, or else he saw the god.[68]

68. *A Voyage to Pagany,* p. 147.

Maybe you changed to the red wheelbarrow, but that's all right.

WILLIAMS. Of course I was in despair of ever seeing "the god." It's the thing that depresses me always. And I need this sort of talk, to give me more courage, to go ahead.

SIEGEL. I hope so.

WILLIAMS. But, you see, nothing happens, nothing seems to happen in the world. We go off by ourselves. But it doesn't seem to happen. All that happens is what's in the newspapers and what's in Korea; and no one realizes that the poem is related to Korea, and related to everything in life. They don't care, and if they don't care—"nothing happens."

SIEGEL. What you're saying is that the poem is related to the original energy of the world which will not be denied.

WILLIAMS. Good. That's fine, that's fine. In other words, you've got to believe it *above* all that, and you sometimes lose faith—well, not faith, you don't lose faith, you lose courage, that's all. And as you get older and your powers become less, you feel—well, what has happened? nothing much.

SIEGEL. Well, I should like to deal with *Paterson* in extenso. And I can say this about that letter, which most of the Society here know: when I saw you write that—I just trembled with it.

WILLIAMS. Well, I felt it.

SIEGEL. Well, but I still tremble.

WILLIAMS. I wrote that very excited. You talk about the volcano: well, of course, we go around sitting on the volcano all the time. And some people have the wrong kind of volcano, and they blow them to hell. But in this terrible feeling of having this volcano in you, and having to discipline it—ink on the page, of a piece of paper, that's a big thing—you just tremble to make that thing stay in there.

SIEGEL. But you've *done* it, that's the point.

WILLIAMS. Yes, but I've been kicked around for it. Because, like the old Baroness said to me, "Dr. Williams, come to me! and I will give you syphilis, and you will be a great man!" I mean that idea that you have to throw yourself into the world, let yourself go, and at the same time you've got to hold yourself down.

SIEGEL. Yes, yes.

WILLIAMS. But you see, it's unsatisfactory. You want to run away, and at the same time you have to stay.

SIEGEL. Well, there's nothing that you endure that a magnet doesn't.

WILLIAMS (*laughs*). Well, you have a lovely large way of putting things. It really is beyond what I see. You do. And I respect it, and I value it.

SIEGEL. Well, I tell you, I should like it if your position as poet—as I said, you're right now the most talked of person writing poetry in America.

WILLIAMS. You think so.

SIEGEL. Yes. I don't go in for schmoozing.

WILLIAMS. No, no; I know. I know that, and I'm not questioning that.

SIEGEL. I'm saying it because I've followed this very carefully. There is a friend of the Society who said, even before we met here, "You know, more people are talking about Williams now than they do of Eliot," and he said it with a customary kind of intensity. And I've noticed it. And the fact that there are these poems in the collected form, and the lectures that you write about. But I'm worrying whether I'm tiring you.

WILLIAMS. No.

SIEGEL. I hope not. Do you want some time to hear some work dealt with more textually?

WILLIAMS. Yes; and not only mine, but I'll come again when you talk about some other poets.

SIEGEL. Would you like to come when I talk on "Hamlet Revisited"?

WILLIAMS. I'd love to!

SIEGEL. You're invited. I believe it'll be two Fridays after the twenty-sixth. Is that all right for you? The Friday after the twenty-sixth will be the twenty-eighth—the Friday after that.

WILLIAMS. I think I could come, I don't know anything that would stop me at all. I'd love to come, I'd enjoy it thoroughly.

SIEGEL. I'd like you to see where some of the rhythms that are in that [*Hamlet*] have a kinship to rhythms here [in Williams].

WILLIAMS. I don't look for that.

SIEGEL. I mean what I say here; I know when there's music in lines, when a person has seen happily the rock bottom and light of things.

WILLIAMS. Yes.

SIEGEL. I know that. It's there; and I just hope that you see that there are many friends you have.

WILLIAMS. After I read *The Sea Around Us,* I feel like I want to shoot myself. That doesn't seem to offer any hope of anything at all. That's just the most depressing book I ever read in my life. It just simply

talks about—just casually—about what the world's
going to be, and it's going to cool off, and everybody's going to be dead. And this part of the world
is going to be 250 feet under water anyhow, all
around New York.

SIEGEL. Well, I have never recommended that book.
In fact, Barbara Lekberg once brought some passages of it from the *New Yorker,* and you remember,
perhaps, that my reception of it wasn't too enthusiastic?

BARBARA LEKBERG. Yes.

WILLIAMS. Those things—well, it is of course the
problem of religion, in a general way. I notice when
you talk about "God or," you say something of that
sort. What is the—

SIEGEL. God is the thing that connects objects. That's
what you're writing about.

WILLIAMS. Yes, but how long do we last, ourselves?
Immortally? It's not our business to ask.

SIEGEL. A person interested in poetry is interested in
the nature of immortality.

WILLIAMS. Yes, he is, very definitely. But he's defeated.

SIEGEL. Well, I'm not saying that. I'm not saying. But
whatever cheerful things I say, I'm not going to say
without any basis. Now I know you're against
sonnets—

WILLIAMS. No, I'm not.

SIEGEL. Well, you say so.

WILLIAMS. I know I do, because you have to say so
in order to throw the other thing into a better light,
that's all. People have the idea that a sonnet is
synonymous with a poem. A lot of people have that:
"A sonnet is The Poem at its highest reach." Well,

hell, it has nothing to do with the poem. And I simply insist that it's one of the things you can do if you happen to want to imitate somebody that did it better than you can ever do it. And if you want to do that—fine. Go ahead, have fun. But there is another—

SIEGEL. Could you mention (pardon me, if you don't mind?)—can you mention one sonnet you've liked?

WILLIAMS. Well, sure. I like many of Shakespeare's sonnets, although they're not the Italian sonnet. Even Wordsworth's on London Bridge—you know, the famous one.

SIEGEL. I know you quote Wordsworth's "The world is too much with us," and you say, "It's not half enough."

WILLIAMS. Yes.

SIEGEL. And do you know what you also do?

WILLIAMS. What?

SIEGEL. You have a motto from Dryden. It's for the last part of the *Autobiography*. You have here:

> Old though I am, for lady's love unfit,
> the power of beauty I remember yet.[69]

WILLIAMS. That's from Chaucer, I never can find it.

SIEGEL. It's not from Chaucer.

WILLIAMS. It's not? My God! Where does that come from?

SIEGEL. It's from the first few lines of Dryden's "Cymon and Iphigenia."

WILLIAMS. My God, no wonder I couldn't find it. I thought it was Chaucer.

69. *Autobiography*, p. 277.

SIEGEL. Martha, have you got that Hazlitt?—Here, I think it's in here.

MARTHA BAIRD. No, that's not it. Here—*Elegant Extracts.*

WILLIAMS. You have such an encyclopedic knowledge of poetry!

SIEGEL. I'm just interested in poetry. Do you want to see it, or shall it be read to you?

WILLIAMS. Read it, I want to hear it. I want to see it besides.

SIEGEL. Lou Dienes, you can take part, you can read it.

LOUIS DIENES *(reads).*

> Old as I am, for ladies' love unfit,
> The power of beauty I remember yet,
> Which once inflamed my soul, and still
>   inspires my wit.[70]

WILLIAMS. Well, it does. That's right to the point.

SIEGEL. It's a retelling of a story from Boccaccio.

WILLIAMS *(looking at the passage).* Oh, it *is* misquoted. "Old *though* I am," I have; it's "Old *as* I am." Well, it was a very real thing to me.

SIEGEL. It's a very fine triplet.

WILLIAMS. Yes, because I certainly do remember it. Well, thank God they didn't put "Chaucer" after it. They left it blank, anyhow.

SIEGEL. Since you're interested, I'm going to ask Martha to read this sonnet, because I think it's the most hopeful thing in Shakespeare nearly. I talked about it a lot. Sonnet 107 of Shakespeare. Could you read it, Martha?

70. As quoted in Hazlitt's *New Elegant Extracts* (London: 1824), p. 242.

MARTHA BAIRD *(reads).*

> Not mine own fears, nor the prophetic soul
> Of the wide world dreaming on things to come,
> Can yet the lease of my true love control,
> Suppos'd as forfeit to a confin'd doom.
> The mortal moon hath her eclipse endur'd,
> And the sad augurs mock their own presage;
> Incertainties now crown themselves assur'd,
> And peace proclaims olives of endless age.
> Now with the drops of this most balmy time
> My love looks fresh, and Death to me subscribes,
> Since, spite of him, I'll live in this poor rhyme,
> While he insults o'er dull and speechless tribes;
>   And thou in this shalt find thy monument,
>   When tyrants' crests and tombs of brass are spent.

SIEGEL. I know it's hard to follow, but I talked a lot about that sonnet.

WILLIAMS. No, no, I followed it.

SIEGEL. Well, I'm glad, but you know sometimes those sonnets are. You see, one of the things I did was to take up all the *Sonnets,* and try to show what they were about, and how the grandest sonnets were on the whole the most joyous.

WILLIAMS. I think that's the key to the whole thing.

SIEGEL. It is.

WILLIAMS. It's wonderful to feel it. There was the man, the one person of all time—that spoke in our language—who had that knack of words, that supreme knack of words. Half his power is just the wonderful words. You almost don't care *what* he says, the words come out so magnificently. I can just listen to them all day long.

SIEGEL. There's also how he went after things. You see, I think that if there is this friendliness, to use the—well, he's Elizabethan—I hope you'll see yourself as friendlier.[71] Sheldon Kranz, do you want to say something?

SHELDON KRANZ. Well, I have been reading Dr. Williams' poetry quite closely, and the thing I am most moved by is that somehow the real purpose of poetry seems to have been achieved. After reading the poems, you get a feeling that the world is more exciting than you thought it was before. And I feel that Dr. Williams' poetry, like all good poetry, does seem to say that the world is exciting and wonderful.

SIEGEL. Nancy Starrels, do you want to say something?

NANCY STARRELS. Yes. One thing I'd like to say is that during the months that you discussed the Shakespeare sonnets and all the other poets that you've discussed, one of the things I've always wished is that some of them could have heard what was said. I feel that it is a very moving occasion to have Dr. Williams hear his work discussed. A general trend in all of his work was made much clearer to me. One of the things that stood out, that I missed very much in the Vivienne Koch book, was this structural good time that you talked of. One sentence you said described very much my feeling about many of the poems: the feeling that if you dig, you'll get to freedom. I also was especially interested in your discussion of *Kora in Hell.*

SIEGEL. I think the author himself underestimated that.

71. This refers to Williams' statement about Elizabethan English, p. 8.

WILLIAMS. It almost struck me as funny. Of course they were improvisations, and they seemed sort of romantic.

SIEGEL. Romantic?

WILLIAMS. Loose statements, they're too loose. I really wrote the thing just as I say: they were improvisations. I tell you just this: at one time, wanting to practice—and it's always a good thing to loosen up the fingers, in anything you're doing, just to let the thing ride, let it flow—I made up my mind I would write something every day, without any knowledge at all of what I was going to say.

SIEGEL. Well, you had a demon by you.

WILLIAMS. There was a demon, all right; yes, there was a demon. But I couldn't capture him, so I thought I'd let him reveal himself.

SIEGEL. A demon with a good ruler.

WILLIAMS. And every night when I came home, I would write, and not look at it; just write and put it in the drawer—

SIEGEL. I guess I should be sorry I did look at it?

WILLIAMS. Just put it down, and put it in the drawer. At the end of the year I threw away a lot of things—maybe I shouldn't have, but I did, because it was too bulky and there was too much there, and sometimes it was just silly, it was nothing. Then of course the comments at the bottom were put in afterwards, because I thought no one would know what I was writing about at all.

SIEGEL. That was during the First World War, apparently. It's a poem of intricate hope.

WILLIAMS. But I've never touched it since, and never read it aloud.

SIEGEL. Sorry: I interfered.

WILLIAMS. No, I suppose I ought to. I've been thinking recently it would be a good hour's talk.

SIEGEL (*showing book*). For those who want to—this is that first edition, the only edition; it's so different from the later poems.—Well, I'll ask Barbara Lekberg to say something, because she represents an art which I—well, talked about.

BARBARA LEKBERG. I was struck by the fury and excitement in the poems, and also the organization. I saw more clearly that it's a problem that is at the basis of sculpture, too. And seeing it solved in the poems this way really taught me a great deal. I was very affected by seeing it.

WILLIAMS. It was very effective. You've opened up a lot of new territory for me.

SIEGEL. So you're going to be here on—April fourth, that will be?

WILLIAMS. I wanted to tell you about that one about Portrait of Myself. That has a queer history. I wrote that very excited—and you read it very well, you probably read it better than any of them, it went off very well, and it really astonished me—but I wrote it, and you know, no one wants to reveal too much of himself. We all dream of being out in the street with the pants off, you know—that's a common dream. And I wrote that thing and—"Uh-uh, no." And I crumpled it up and threw it in the wastebasket. Bob McAlmon was in the house at the time, and he fished it out, and showed it. Well.

SIEGEL. That's a very good thing, it's got love and mathematics. That's a combination.—So I hope we see each other, then, the first Friday in April. I'm going to talk on *Hamlet*.

3

Letters and Journals
March 1952–December 1957

Part Three

FROM MARTHA BAIRD'S 1952 JOURNAL

Wednesday, March 5, continued. During the talk Williams was just the way he should be: so right and so unexpected, like a poem. The way he sits is very graceful: easy, yet attentive. (Norse, I should say, came a little late. What happened to Gascoyne I do not know.)

Then afterwards he meets everyone, and is so gracious, and autographs Barbara Singer's copy of his poems for her. She doesn't ask him, he just sees it and says, "I suppose you'd like me to put my name in this?" And she says, "Well, since you mention it."

He says he hasn't written a poem in years. ES says, "Do you mind if I encourage you?" He says, "You already have."

So he leaves, and finally everyone leaves. When we are alone, E. is almost crying again. He says: "What he could *see!* My God, what he could *see!*"

Saturday, March 8. A letter to "Eli" from "Bill." It is one of his queer letters, on terrible paper. He says after all, Wednesday was just talk. But he says E. gives him a feeling of blessedness. Then he says E. is like John the Baptist in the wilderness, but he's in danger of submerging himself. Then he cautions him about giving feelings to a river in a poem—says: Watch that.

E. is in a quandary as to how to answer it. I say it is just a simple letter (well, it is not simple), the kind of letter you don't have to answer. But E. says Williams is asking for something in this letter, and he knows what it is in a general way but not in a specific way. He says all in all, he feels there is something going on he doesn't see. Do I have any idea what it is? Well, I feel there is something going on we don't see, either; but I don't know what it is.

Williams says in this letter he is really going to get down to E.'s poems now. Apparently he has read only those he read before the first letter, which was the first group mimeographed. Then he has read those which have been sent in letters. He's enthusiastic about all of them except the "Marriage Poem" and the one about the river, and wants E. to read all of them at the Museum of Modern Art. He hasn't said anything about having read the lecture on "Poetry and Technique" or *The Aesthetic Method*. He wants to hear ES *talk* on other poets, but he doesn't seem to want to read what he has said. Isn't there something queer here? From that first letter, wouldn't you think he'd want to read everything of ES's he could? E. says Williams seems to be afraid of those poems.

And wouldn't you think he'd want to talk more to ES? Wouldn't you? He accepts eagerly our invitations, but we are afraid to give too many, without any from him.

There is a feeling of some kind of reserve, unspoken, perhaps unseen; and it is in such contrast to his manner, which is so open, so enthusiastic, so generous, so dear.

It is queer.

I am also surprised that E. doesn't know what is going on. I am touched that he doesn't, and also that he tries so humbly to find out from me if I've seen something he hasn't. I wish I had.

Also he says if he knew what Williams felt when he read those poems, he'd know what to say to him now: how he wishes he knew just what he felt! He says he has a feeling that he is dealing with something very deep and primitive. I don't understand this, but this is what he said.

ELI SIEGEL TO W. C. WILLIAMS

March 10, 1952

Dear Bill:

I guess we have much to say to each other, and the question is, how to say it. Mistakes can so easily be made when conversation or letter-writing goes places.

There is poetry in you still looking for a way to show itself. How much this means. How you want to love earth! How you want to love things! If you can show this love, even more than you have, well, it will be mighty good. Whatever else my talk of last Wednesday may have done, I hope it was Spring-and-all-ish.

So you want to see earth a certain way.

Maybe we can talk sometime on how earth and ourselves should be seen.

I think criticism is poetry in the long run. Matthew Arnold said, Poetry is a criticism of life. This is somewhat right.

I have some wishes for you. I wish you could like George Saintsbury as much as I do, and what he stands for. (I enclose a poem getting him in.) If I am submerged, I wish you would encourage me not to be. I wish you would like our having met, more and more. I wish you would never take back one nice, true thing you have ever felt—even in 1886 or 1904. (I like the word *nice:* it is greatly silly.)

I should like for you to hear talks of mine on such fellow-poets of yours as Samuel Taylor Coleridge, Emily Dickinson, John Donne, Robert Burns, Edmund Spenser, William Butler Yeats, James Stephens, Charles Pierre Baudelaire, Christina Rossetti, Vachel Lindsay—and oh so on, wherever truth may take us. In all this I say again what I said Wednesday: there's a way you have of seeing our terrible friend, reality, that makes you as definite as the world itself, as definite as you. You are a sharp flower. You are: seeing. You stand for seeing. You are you-seeing.

I wrote the poem about the river and heart in 1933. A river is something you have used a great deal to say what you see with. And I thought that in the 1933 poem about the beating heart and the flowing river, there was a relation good to look at. The word *pleased* is used in the sense that the body is pleased when it has food come to it, the skin is pleased when warmth comes to it; or, even, earth is pleased when plants find their way through it. So I'm a hylozoist; so I may be wrong. Yet I shouldn't like it if I felt rivers could be pleased in no way at all. With all this, critically you could be right. Down with needless subjectivity.

The line in the poem "It Stays Because It Is So Much" you couldn't make out a word of, is:

A line is a mingling of going and staying.

That poem I thought I might read during the talk to show what I saw line as; but it didn't come in.

I'm not sure about the time I have in the Museum reading. Certainly, I should like to get in two shorter poems and "Hot Afternoons." Martha and I will time the reading of these: I don't want to do anything disproportionate.

Martha has written something about her first knowing of me, and of me as a philosophic critic once of her. Would you like to see this writing? It is factual, honest and beautiful, and makes me less unknown.

Little Couplet

When we are cactus and crocus,
There's something in us to choke us.

Come to me now these lines of James Stephens:

What could one say to her? There are no words
That one could say to her![1]

(I think much of James Stephens. I discussed much his "The Red-Haired Man's Wife.")

But there are words one can say to you. May I say to you with some passion, Oh Bill! make it clearer you want to hear them. Make it clearer the time is a good time.

However it may be, there is March 26—such a date

---

1. From "Deirdre."

—and there is April 4, 1952, when William Carlos Williams—poet discussed wherever poetry is discussed in America, in whatever state, and in foreign lands, too—because of kind, welcome statement of his—is expected to hear Eli Siegel talk on "Hamlet Revisited; or, The Family Should Be Poetry," at the home of Martha and Eli Siegel.

Edifying Triplet

May you see all you want to see,
May you be all you want to be,
And so, true prosperitee.

So, somewhat scared, and sincerely,
ELI

FROM MARTHA BAIRD'S 1952 JOURNAL

Sunday, March 23. We talk about the Museum of Modern Art event. E. says what it means, to read that poem again, after so many years—it's almost like Lazarus, risen from the dead. He says sometimes he's afraid of how much emotion he has. He mentions how he almost cried when he saw Williams here that Wednesday. We talk of things that may possibly happen. I have had apprehensions: that Williams may be quite different from how he has been heretofore, that he won't act like the person who wrote the letter, that he may be rude even. (He hasn't answered that last letter E. sent him, the one I felt was beautiful.) To my surprise, E. says what he's afraid of is if Williams is too nice, or if he gets kind of sentimental and confused in a sweet way. He's afraid if that happens, it'll set all kinds of thoughts of the past, and the paradoxes, and the injustice and the justice, and the praise and the disrespect—it'll set all that working in him and he won't want to read. He says he'd rather read other poems than "Hot Afternoons," anyway; reading that one is almost too much.

He said once if anybody was really fair to him, he thinks he'd faint.

EDITORS' NOTE. *A transcript of the March 5 lecture and discussion was sent to Williams with the following letter.*

ELI SIEGEL TO W. C. WILLIAMS

March 23, 1952

Dear Bill:

We shall see each other on Wednesday. Meantime here is a record of the lovely event on March 5, this year.

How truth and like of it can go with spring.

I hope that more can be said and I hope that the unsaid is grand and kind.

Surely we hope that this Wednesday will be as fine and deep a Wednesday as the March 5 one.

Salutations to Ginny. May the mss. enclosed meet a desire of yours.

Sincerely,
ELI

FROM MARTHA BAIRD'S 1952 JOURNAL

Monday, March 24. E. has a long conversation with Nat Herz on the phone. Much to my surprise, he asks Nat if he thinks he should wear a white shirt or a colored one to the Museum? Nat about falls out of the telephone booth at this, I gather, but he says he thinks a white one.

They talk a lot about poetry and how to see it. Towards the end, something that moves me a great deal is that E. says thirty years ago or so, when he used to feel very confused sometimes, he'd think of an unspoiled bit of sky, or a good line, or a baby not yet born, and it would make the confusion more bearable. Other people, when they're confused, will think about past personal triumphs of their own to console themselves, but E. would think of something not himself, something in the world.

Tuesday, March 25. This afternoon a man called from the *Baltimore Sun.* Name of Catling. Said he'd already talked to Williams and he was "glowing." Asked ES why he didn't get published? And wanted to know the titles of the poems he was reading. E. said Catling also was interested in seeing the talk on Williams, and maybe I should send him a copy; also a copy of Williams' letter.

Late in the evening, he reads some *Hamlet* to me. This helps. Also he writes himself a poem, giving himself advice. He says if he expresses some of the emotion now, maybe it will be in better control tomorrow.[2]

2. The poem was "Let the Seeing Go On." It appears in *Hot Afternoons,* p. 61.

Thursday, March 27. Well, it is now something that happened.

E. wore his brown suit, white shirt, red tie, and new topcoat. I wore my light coat and my tweed suit. We went into the subway and then got off, and there was the Museum looking awfully big. The lobby was sort of dimly lighted, with people milling about in it, among whom I recognized Sheldon Kranz.

The auditorium is also bigger than I remembered, and it didn't seem very full. The stage looked good. A great big gorgeous modern table, with six of those chairs behind it—modern of course—looking like washtubs. And to the right a stand with a microphone. From the front it looks like a slab of solid walnut. Beautiful.

Dorothy Koppelman said she saw Williams come in, and she heard some girls say Oscar Williams was there.

Finally, the poets all came out, and sat in their chairs. They all had on white shirts, just as Nat said. Then a man in a tux with a well-modulated voice said a few eulogistic things of Williams: this was Monroe Wheeler.

Then Williams got up and said, "I hope you will remember you are in the *Modern* Museum," and looked fixedly at the audience, a little in the manner of Lionel Barrymore. Then he said a few general things about poetry and modernity in America. Then he began to talk about the New Poets. ES he talked about first. He was conservative. He didn't say anything to make E. cry, which I suppose was good, but I confess I was a little disappointed. He said he was from New York, that he had "lived inconspicuously" and was doing fine work with his "Symposium for Aesthetic Realism," and that he was a *new* poet.

Then Williams said a little something about the other people. He said Kenneth Beaudoin comes from a very old family and it is good to see an American "of that vintage" doing new things. He said a lyric of David Lougee's had struck him and he'd said, "That's the boy for me." He said Harold Norse was from Pennsylvania, and a little something else. And Stanley Lawrence Berne, he said, writes these "verbalisms" which he thinks "ought to be heard."

He did them all in a row, and by the time he got to the end, you didn't know which was which; and when they read, you didn't know which was which either.

ES got up to read, and first he read "Meant To Be"; and he made a little comment which was graceful and definite. He said the poem was from this year. Then he said he was going to read one from 1928 which was earthy. This got a little laugh, from the way he said it. Then he read "She's Crazy and It Means Something." Then he said he had a short poem, written very seriously, which Louis Untermeyer got into an anthology as the shortest poem in the world without acknowledging him as the author, and he had been very much hurt by this. So he said: "I—/ Why?" Then he did the one about the line, "It Stays Because It Is So Much," which he said Dr. Williams had designated. Then he said that "Montana" was the only poem ever used for streetcar advertising: "Hot Afternoons Are Not in Bay Shore." And he read it.

There was a lot of applause. It seemed as if people wanted to call for more—but they were decorous, and didn't. After all, there were four more people to read.

Then E. sat down in his bathtub chair again and listened to the others. He really listened, too: you could see.

After they had all read, Williams got up and said this had been new, and the value of it wasn't to be judged yet, and whether it had been worth anything or not was up to us to see.

And that was all!

Ten minutes of ten, and it was over.

Then we went into the lobby, and people congratulated ES. We saw Ginny, and she introduced us to Mrs. Williams. I was surprised by her: a very thin, frail old lady.

E. said the reading needed more of a spirit of controversy, and some participation by the audience. He said this to Williams too—Williams asked him. He didn't seem too happy tonight, WCW.

I was ready to go home, but E. wants to go to the reception. So we walk across town to 242 East 52nd Street, where is Mrs. Rockefeller's Guest House.

There are a lot of people standing about, most of whom I'd seen at the Museum, and a big punch bowl, and everybody has little punch glasses. We see the Williamses a little, but they are going to leave early.

Ginny says they got the typed copy of ES's talk on WCW (we mailed it to him hoping he'd get it before this night) and she was very impressed by it, and Mrs. Williams was reading it. Ginny was more talkative than she has been before. E. says he is sorry for chiding her for smoking at the Williams talk (he is nearsighted and didn't know it was she: just glared in her direction). She says, Oh, *she's* sorry, and got scolded for it all the next day. She says she has two children and is a terrible mother. She says again she likes *The Aesthetic Method*. E. says would she like to read something on the child from an aesthetic point of view? She says yes.

Williams has a new job: Consultant on American Poetry for the Library of Congress, and they're going to move to Washington. This seems terrible to me: for him to leave that place he's lived in all his life and go where there are all those crooks. Ginny defends the idea, saying he'll have more time to write and lecture, and he shouldn't have to practice medicine now. That is true, he shouldn't.

EDITORS' NOTE. *Friday, April 4 was the date of Eli Siegel's lecture, "Hamlet Revisited." At the Museum of Modern Art, Williams had said again that he was coming. But he neither came to the lecture nor sent any message of explanation.*

Saturday, April 5. E. says he is worried about Williams and wants to call him up. This is the first time he has done that.

I took notes of the conversation as follows:

"This is Eli Siegel. . . . You know, we were expecting you yesterday . . . I'm sorry . . . people were looking for you. You are well, though? . . . You're not angry about anything? If you are, I can stand it. . . . I can understand that. . . . What do you suggest I do now? About our meetings, our communications. What do you think I should do? . . . Sure, sure. . . . I got a letter from Huntington Cairns today. He's in the National Gallery at Washington. I've known him a long time. He knows about your going to the Library of Congress. . . . Everybody knows about you. . . . Do you want to see us again? We could come to see you if it were easier. . . . You've been one of my best friends. You know, when I came down here, there were tears in my eyes?[3] . . . Whether you come here or not isn't the point. . . . I want us to feel we're for each other where we begin. . . . There is something I don't want to lose as to you. Don't mind being senti-mental . . ."

It seems Williams asked E. if he could call him. E. said yes, any time. He asked if he could call some time and say he'd like to come the next day. E. said sure. E. said Williams said he just couldn't get here yester-day; he's been depressed.

E. talks to him very sweetly, not as if he were hurt or angry or disappointed. He is not. He *expects* these things. But why *should* he? Why should he?

He says it was just too much for Williams. The talk on his poems, then the transcript of the talk, then E.'s letter, then the Museum thing which seems to have affected him a lot, and then *Hamlet*. It was just too much. He reminds me that I have my quotas: some-times I can listen for an hour, and then some capacity is reached. He says he didn't space these invitations right, and now he knows better.

3. This refers to the night of March 5; see p. 31.

Monday, April 7. A letter from Williams, so sad, so badly typed, it makes for tears. He says he may be getting another cerebral hemorrhage: twenty-four hours will tell. But he doesn't want E. to feel he's neglectful.

E. calls up again and speaks to the nurse, Miss Hampton. She says he is not so well, but he is not so ill either—he didn't have a stroke or anything.

E. says do I feel bad now for being so mad at him? I say I wasn't mad at him, I was disappointed; I was mad at Ginny, though—she could have called.

E. says do I see how important it is to be kind?

ELI SIEGEL TO W. C. WILLIAMS

April 7, 1952

Dear Bill Williams:
Write more poems yet.
Sycamores forever.
Change bother into the roughness every line has.
—Dearly,
Eli

*   *   *   *

FROM MARTHA BAIRD'S 1954 JOURNAL

Entry of 9-22-54, recapitulating events of 1954. A University of Indiana magazine, *The Folio,* had wanted to print four of ES's poems and WCW's letter.[4] A few

4. A section of the letter had been quoted by Nat Herz in an article about "Hot Afternoons Have Been in Montana" which appeared in *Poetry,* under the title "Communication," in the August 1952 issue. Karl Shapiro was then editor.

months later, they wrote saying WCW had refused permission to quote the letter "either in whole or in part," and sent back all the poems.

It was a cruel blow. I resolved not to tell ES.

I did write to my father about it, though. His response surprised me very much, and restored my faith in him.

He was very indignant: impersonally indignant. He reread Williams' letter and said, how could the man write that and then behave this way? He said we should go see him and ask for an explanation. And he sent me $100 for "expenses."

I took Nancy Starrels into my confidence and we discussed it all: what to do, and how, and why this all happened, and what it means, anyhow.

The Indiana letters were made more puzzling by the fact that about the same time, I had some correspondence with John Thirlwall of the CCNY English Department, who was working on a volume of Williams' letters and was interested in seeing this one. He wrote very warmly about it and said Dr. Williams remembers it very well.

What I finally did was to write WCW a letter, saying nothing about the Indiana business, but asking his permission to use the letter as an introduction to ES's poems. I wrote two letters: one short, one long. Then I had to decide which to send. I felt I should take the responsibility and I didn't even want Nancy to see the letters, but she helped me very much. She asked me what was in the long one, and I told her a little, and she said, Oh, let me see it. So I did, and she read it, and wiped her eyes a little, and said —SEND IT!

So then we both cried, and I signed it, and put a special delivery stamp on it, and we both went out together and put it in the mailbox. This was June 9, the day before my thirty-third birthday.

Concurrently with this, and while the matter of the letter was very much on my mind, I did something else which for me was very brave. I felt I couldn't *stand* ES's poems not being published, and I decided to call up Houghton Mifflin in Boston and ask them if they were sincere when they said they liked them but couldn't afford to publish them, because if it was a matter of money, I would guarantee them against loss. So, after the Memorial Day weekend I called Mr. Olney. He didn't bat an eye. He remembered the poems immediately, though it was two years ago since they sent them back. He said very politely that they hadn't been sincere: if they like something enough they publish it regardless of the money, and they don't do any "subsidized" publishing at all. But he suggested I send the poems again, and they'd be treated as a new manuscript.

I felt it would be very good if I could tell him the Williams letter could be used as an introduction, so I was doubly eager to hear from Williams.

MARTHA BAIRD TO W. C. WILLIAMS

June 9, 1954

Dear William Carlos Williams:

Houghton Mifflin is at present considering the manuscript of Eli Siegel's poems, for the second time. I have hopes that they will publish them.

In February, it will be thirty years since the first appearance of "Hot Afternoons." This thought is much on my mind these days: thirty years, and not one book has been published. It is cruel and wasteful! It is shameful!

I have resolved, if it is in my power, a book is going to appear before next February. If an established publisher won't undertake it, I shall (with assistance) have it printed by Definition Press.

My purpose in writing to you is to ask your permission to use your letter to me (of November 3, 1951) as an introduction to the poems when they appear, by whomever published—either by itself, or incorporated in a longer preface. I am sure it will help immensely, both with the publishers, and later with reviewers and readers.

I have worked on a preface which I shall send for your approval or comment, if you wish. It began as an introduction Nat Herz wrote for a reading of ES's poems last winter. I changed it some and added to it, and have included the most important passages of your letter.

I am not sure this is the best way. Perhaps your letter by itself would be better. Certainly, "Preface by W. C. Williams" would be more impressive on the dustjacket than "Preface by N. Herz and M. Baird."

I have always felt the letter was as great a credit to you as it is to him. I remember how you spoke of it when you were here in January and in March 1952—as if you were proud of it, and that any way it could be used to help the poems, you were for.

It does seem strange, after all that happened, and after the great warmth that was shown on those oc-

casions, that there should have been this long silence.
I should like to act as if it hadn't happened—to be
immediately and continuously in the atmosphere of
March 5, 1952, when Eli talked about your poems, and
when—or I never saw anything true in my life—the
true WCW saw the true ES and was seen by him.
Yet I know how hard it is to be faithful to one's best
emotions, to one's keenest seeings. ES makes extraordinary demands on another self, just by being what he
is. You knew this when you said:

> The mind that made that mark is a different mind
> from ours. It is following different incentives. The
> eyes back of it are new eyes. They are seeing some-
> thing different from ours.

He is so much, so good—so honest, kind, and smart
—so beautiful, that the ordinary ego can't stand it. I
understand this very well, and have suffered from it
myself. If you knew how many times I have retreated
and contracted, and then felt ashamed.

I know how hard it is, and how baseless and silly
sometimes can seem the finest things one has ever
felt. Yet one asks it of oneself to be true to that. I
have seen the same difficulty many times with other
people too.

So when I say that ES, as he is, so humble and so
great, is more than most egos can stand, I am speaking
from a great deal of experience.

You hinted at this in your letter, when you spoke
of "the extreme resentment that the fixed, sclerotic mind
feels confronting this new." That is certainly true;
yet something of the "fixed sclerotic" is in all of us.
It is a most contradictory thing: the sight ES offers

of the world—through his poems, through his teaching, through himself—is something we long for so much that when we see it, it seems too good to be true. The part of oneself that is close to art is so pleased, so delighted, so grateful. But the *other* part, the unrelated ego, is affronted and insulted. ES, by his existence, seems to imply that we are not perfect as we are, that we have something to learn, and that he can teach it.

You, having the artist so much in you, were affected in the first way to an extraordinary degree. Perhaps later the second reaction took place, in a way that may not even have been recognized?

I have searched my mind for some other explanation of the cessation which began after the Museum of Modern Art event and after the talk ES gave on your poems which pleased you so much—do you remember?—you said: "It's as if everything I've ever done has been for you."

I have even thought that maybe some unfriendly person told you something untrue about ES to make you dislike him. But if that had happened, would you believe such a person without seeking any explanation from ES? No; not unless some resentment was already working.

I believe that:

1. What you wrote in that letter is TRUE.
2. What you felt when ES discussed your poems is TRUE.
3. There is something you want to see: he knows what it is.
4. There is something you want to know: he can teach you how.

It is not just about poetry, though it began with poetry. It is about the way things are; it is about the reality of things and the art in things—including people. It is about the meaning of life, and death, and immortality. It is about how form and substance are the same.

I cannot tell it to you, but I have seen enough to know that ES can. I see some things you don't, and more clearly; but in other respects you are way ahead of me, because you are a Real Artist.

Maybe the situation is too incongruous—that you, the internationally admired poet and doctor should want ES to be your teacher (your letter implied this, though it did not state it). It does look incongruous. The whole thing is incongruous; it is nearly incredible; it is almost heartbreaking.

Here he is—with the most beautiful mind in the world. It is at its finest. He has worked for years to get it this way—to organize it, polish it, keep it pure. It is ready. It is at its peak. He should be the teacher of the whole world—and here he is, pouring out all those riches for thirty or forty people on Jane Street.

You said he had received opposition and then neglect, "due not to resentment but by the sheer inability of the general mind to grasp what has taken place." That is true; yet the people who come to Jane Street represent the "general mind." Nancy Starrels, Sheldon Kranz, Barbara Lekberg, Mr. and Mrs. Robbins—you met them. They are not geniuses, or remarkable in any way, except perhaps through destiny. But they all have the same inward conviction, arrived at not through any conspiracy, but through the secret searching of each one's soul: that Eli Siegel is a great man

—great in our century and in the history of the world. Why do they think this? Who forced them to? No one. They are compelled to think it because of the irresistible evidence of their experience; because of the force of the effect of his words, his logic, his way of seeing, on them.

They are half proud of this effect, and half ashamed of it—because, after all, who is he in the eyes of the world that they should honor him so much? He has no backing, no position, no reputation, no marble halls, no books published. He hasn't even an impressive manner. He just acts honest.

That is why, even when they do speak for him, they lack conviction in the fullest sense.

That is why what you wrote is so important: you are the first person, qualified to speak, who has spoken out.

I am not so naive as to believe that one book of poems is going to make everything easy from now on. But I feel that one book of poems, properly published and launched, with your words as preface, will make a decisive difference. It will be a break in the horrible brassy wall.

He is very courageous. He is very good. He does not even have a bad disposition in private. What do you think of that? He is full of humor and interest in everything; yet I feel there is a great sadness in him, and a great loneliness. Sometimes he says: Won't anybody see me as I am? Won't anybody be glad I know what I do, *all the time?*

He said once that most of his confidence has come from himself, but there have been three times when he got confidence from the outside world: 1, was the

Nation prize; 2, was from me, when I was so happy because of what he taught me (that is true, and that is why he married me—because when he criticized me, I liked it—I haven't always lived up to this, though); and the third thing was your letter.

Another thing he told me was that he loved you more than any other man.

Yours truly,

MARTHA BAIRD SIEGEL

Entry of 9-22-54, continued. I heard nothing. So I called up Mr. Thirlwall to find out if W. was still in Rutherford—maybe he hadn't got the letter. But he was. So unless his family intercepted it, he must have gotten it. After two weeks, Nancy wrote him a note, very tactful, saying she would call him in two or three days and ask for an appointment to talk to him.

Then he answered. A very short note with a very shaky signature. But he said we could use the letter and he wished ES good luck. So he *didn't* take it back.

Then I wrote to Mr. Olney again, but in a few weeks they returned the poems anyway.

Still, we have his written permission to use the letter, and as time passed, that seemed more and more important.[5]

✿   ✿   ✿   ✿

FROM MARTHA BAIRD'S 1957 JOURNAL

Friday, February 15. Hot Afternoons is going to be published by Definition Press. I am getting the manu-

5. The letter was printed for the first time in its entirety in the October-December 1956 issue of *Poetry Public*, edited by Lawrence Richard Holmes.

script ready, with duplicates. I figure 128 pages, at least. Marvin Mondlin will be business manager. I like the way he talks very much—it is both eager and sober.

Monday, March 4. Hot Afternoons goes to the printer: it is to be Clarke & Way.

Sunday, March 24. We have just proofread the first four galleys of *Hot Afternoons,* and it is a lovely sunny day.

We have had a whole thing with David Way about whether the run-over lines should be justified or not. In the sample pages he justified them, but when the proofs came, they were unjustified. It looked sort of ragged to us. But he has a Reason; and it is not a technical printers' reason, it is an artistic, poetic reason. He said he feels there is a precision and exactness in the use of words in these poems which is different, and stretching the space out to justify the lines does not honor this precision. It's all right for Whitman and Sandburg, he says, because they write a kind of sprawling line anyway; but not Siegel. Also, he says, this book is "definitive" and we don't have to follow conventions: we are making a new thing, with laws unto itself. Also, he says, his partner, Bert Clarke, knew the title poem from years ago and thinks the book is "long overdue." And he says they feel their press is honored to be printing it.

So we proofread it this morning, a lovely sunny Sunday morning. I am so moved to see "Ralph Isham" in this good type—more than "Hot Afternoons," which I associate with being in print; but "Ralph Isham" I never saw in print before. And there he is: he looks permanent. I think of the line "And his name is not heard in Topeka," and I think now his name *will* be heard in Topeka.

Entry of 8-10-57, recapitulating events. Hot Afternoons is a success. It is the biggest success we ever had. More good things have happened in the last two months than have happened in the whole history of Aesthetic Realism.

The first sign that things were going to go well was when William Cole, of Knopf, who had ordered the book, called up Marvin and said he liked it so much, he wanted to help us if he could. Then he wrote notes to a lot of literary people asking them to give it a mention if they could; and he sent us a carbon of his note and a list of people we should send the book to.

Out of his efforts, we got on television—twice. Leon Pearson's program. He read two poems ("Worms Go South" and "Poem on Lagoons") and the fact that a book of *poems* was talked about on TELEVISION impressed people greatly. The days he talked about it were June 9 and June 16.

In between Leon Pearson's broadcasts came John Henry Faulk on CBS. This was the most remarkable thing—*Hot Afternoons* on television and radio, but nothing in print! Lou Robbins had given the book to Faulk, and Faulk really liked it. He told Lou Robbins it was the first book of poems he'd liked in years, and Mr. Siegel must have a wonderful mind. Faulk's broadcast was on June 13, about 5:30 in the afternoon, and Lou Robbins took a recording of it. He spoke with real feeling, and said Eli Siegel had "touched the very heartbeat of the spirit of America" and that "he makes a man glad he's alive."

Soon after this, Marvin Mondlin went to Chicago and went to lots of bookstores and sold lots of copies. The combination, he said, of W. C. Williams and John Henry Faulk was irresistible.

Oscar Williams' *Silver Treasury of Light Verse* came out about this time with "I—/ Why?" in it, under the title of "The Shortest Poem in the World," and that was very handy. He is a crumb, though, that Oscar Williams. He put in two parodies of the poem —perfectly stupid things—which dull its impact greatly.

We have found that "I—/ Why?" is in three other anthologies (besides Untermeyer's), all without the author's name. In a book by Zillman, of Seattle; in *The Hollow Reed* by Wrinn; and in Herzberg's *Off to Arcady.*

David Way knows Oscar Williams (he printed Gene Derwood's book) and he told Marvin he asked OW: "What's going to happen with *Hot Afternoons?*" and OW said: "Nothing." The way that Way told this to Marvin shows something about the other side of his character, too.

Then in one week, we got two postcards: one from Kenneth Rexroth saying he'd "got it for the *Times*" —meaning he had been asked to review *Hot Afternoons* for the *Times;* and one from Selden Rodman saying he was reviewing it for the *Saturday Review* and we should send him a photo and some biographical information.

On June 30, the *Times* printed a poem from the book, "Notes on the Telephone," in the Poets' Column, and we were very set up by this. No more boycott. No more the brassy wall of silence. This made me more sanguine about the coming Rexroth review.

All this time nothing has been heard from Baltimore. We sent review copies to the *Sun*—nothing. ES wrote to James Bready—nothing. Huntington Cairns ordered a copy of the book very early, but wrote nothing. Definition Press put an ad in the *Sun*, and they loused it up and didn't send proofs or anything. Letters were sent to some Baltimore bookshops and to the library there—nothing.

One day we got—in the same mail—an order for twenty copies from Farrell's in Berkeley, with a letter saying he usually handles only out of print books, but *this* is an exception. Also a letter from Dudley Fitts, at Phillips Andover Academy, saying he likes the book, will recommend it everywhere, and will speak for it to the Bollingen jury of which he is a member.

Tuesday, August 13. I had told Marvin to bring the *Saturday Review* before class. When they come in, I know by the sound of their voices and the looks on their faces that we are in it and it is something good.

I see the headline on the page: "The Spell of a 'Natural,'" it says. Then there is ES's picture: "Full of surprises," it says.

Rodman tells how he was prejudiced in the beginning, on account of Williams' superlatives. Then he describes what he went through as he read the book, putting down his notations. They are all contradictory. Then he says he was "won over in spite of himself."

The last part is the best: "Then he comes up with poems like 'Dear Birds, Tell This to Mothers,' 'She's Crazy and It Means Something,' and 'The World of the Unwashed Dish' which say more (and more movingly) about here and now than any contemporary poems I have read."

It seems still unbelievable. It looks so simple—as if, how else could it be? But what hours of work, what acres of longing preceded it! And there was no small fuss in the *Saturday Review* office, either—they had to get two review copies and two pictures before this finally came to be!

There is "The World of the Unwashed Dish." Everyone is picking out that poem now; but I remember when *Poetry* rejected it. And "Dear Birds." I remember when ES wrote it, on a little pad, in handwriting you could hardly read, after a letter from my mother, the spring before she died. It was really written to her, and I sent it to her, but she wouldn't say anything about it. And then Theodora Harmon got it printed in a little PTA publication in Brooklyn and it fell like a stone in a well. And here is Selden Rodman saying it is one of the most moving contemporary poems he has read.

*   *   *   *

Saturday, December 28. I decide I'll look at good old *Publishers' Weekly* and see what's doing in the book business. There are a lot of ads for Crown in the front, which I read. Then an ad for the National Book Awards. I just let my eye run over the list of books, my judgment for the moment suspended, not hoping much, not fearing much, but with a sense of preparation for disappointment—and my eye sees:

HOT AFTERNOONS HAVE
BEEN IN MONTANA
Eli Siegel

It is *there!* Of eight books nominated for the award, our dear *Hot Afternoons* is one! I didn't expect the announcement until January, and I expected that, should we be among those nominated, we'd get a notification. I never expected just to find it in *Publishers' Weekly.*

It deserves to be there, and it is there. I feel very quiet, very happy. The happiness is great, but at the center of it, there seems to be this quietness. I think that when one is greatly moved, one does not shout.

EDITORS' NOTE ON EVENTS OF *1957-1958* TOUCHING W. C. WILLIAMS. *While all this was occurring with the poems of Eli Siegel, W. C. Williams was silent.*

1. On May 30, 1957, a copy of Hot Afternoons Have Been in Montana: Poems *was sent to Williams. It was not acknowledged.*

2. The Selected Letters of William Carlos Williams, *edited by John C. Thirlwall, was also published in 1957. Williams' letter about Siegel was not included.*

3. This same year, Kora in Hell *was reissued by City Lights Books. In the new introduction, Williams speaks of this book as "an intensely private avowal," "more or less of a secret document for my own wonder and amusement known to few others." There is no mention of Eli Siegel.*

4. *In* I Wanted to Write a Poem, *edited by Edith Heal (Boston: Beacon Press, 1958), Williams is quoted as speaking of* Kora in Hell *as "a unique book, not like any other I have written. It is the one book I have enjoyed referring to more than any of the others. It reveals myself to me and perhaps that is why I have kept it to myself" (p. 26). And: "Perhaps this is the first thing to show me to be a prose writer. As far as can be told, it is the first piece of continuous prose I remember writing" (p. 31). Again, there is no mention of Siegel.*

5. *After June 1954, when Williams gave permission for the use of his letter, there was no word from Williams to Siegel, nor as far as can be ascertained did Williams mention Siegel in any public way whatever. In letters and poems written after March 5, 1952, subjects and ideas Siegel had spoken of to him are alluded to, but Siegel's name is absent.*

4

Supplementary Documents
by Eli Siegel
1955–1967

Part Four

T. S. ELIOT AND W. C. WILLIAMS:

A DISTINCTION

"The Love Song of J. Alfred Prufrock" may still be regarded as representative of Eliot. Later writings like *The Waste Land* and *Four Quartets* have tended to set it off, rather than put it aside. The critical question about "Prufrock"—as about all poems—is: What was the state of mind, or state of being, which made for the choice and placing of the words in the poem? In criticizing a poem, one must criticize the state of mind from which the poem came. To be more exact, let us take some lines:

There will be a time to murder and create,
And time for all the works and days of hands
That lift and drop a question on your plate;
Time for you and time for me,
And time yet for a hundred indecisions,
And for a hundred visions and revisions,
Before the taking of a toast and tea.

Appeared in *The University of Kansas City Review*, October 1955.

Clearly, there is a craftsman working in these lines. However, is there the craftsmanship akin to the organizing force to be felt in a mountain, a crystal, an onion, a fountain? Is there the craftsmanship akin to that of the Psalms and Rimbaud, or akin to the insufficiently impelled craftsmanship of James Russell Lowell and Austin Dobson?

This is not the place to point out inaccuracies of phraseology in these lines of Eliot (there are many in the poem): I must content myself for the while with saying that: "And time for all the works and days of hands/ That lift and drop a question on your plate" is an expression imaginatively untrue; that "works and days of hands" do not, with poetic usefulness, "drop a question on your plate." The important matter is, whether the lines arose from a state simultaneously of lucidity and excitement—from an intense state, so intense that verbal architecture supervened.

Now as to Williams. There is the poem "Young Sycamore." It does not have the mobile tessellation, or something, of "Prufrock." It is a more "naive" poem. Yet, in the deepest sense, there is more art in the Williams work. This is so, because, while in "Prufrock" the arrangement does not arise from heat or from glow, in "Young Sycamore" there is a cunning artistry of itself arising from a glowing, stirred state of mind.

Take the poem's beginning:

> I must tell you
> this young tree
> whose round and firm trunk
> between the wet

> pavement and the gutter
> (where water
> is trickling) rises
> bodily[1]

—the thing seen and the music work at once. And there is a true complexity in the thing seen: what's seen changes to touch. The whole poem is really about the logic of a tree—about the accuracy of sincere energy. The poem is about simplicity altering into opulence.

The lines I have quoted are an instance of visual adequacy and intensity taking the form of words that have syllabic propriety and wonder. A declarative sentence has been divided dramatically and resonantly. Things like this happen in Mother Goose and successful folk poetry: art is there.

When Eliot places words, he places them as dominoes may be placed on a table; when Williams places words—at least often when he does so—he places them as an accurate something places peas in a pod or leaves on a tree.

Is there a difference of source in Williams' "The Red Wheelbarrow" from that of Eliot's "Ash Wednesday"? I believe there is. One need not go as far as Plato (the *Ion*) in thinking that the poet is an immediate representative of aroused and impelling divinity: yet Plato is somewhat right. "The Red Wheelbarrow" of Williams, in its diminutive might, apprehends the wonder and make-up of reality, and the

1. Siegel's earlier discussion of "Young Sycamore" is on pp. 54-55.

apprehension, though rapt—indeed religious in the best sense—is subtly sure of itself and is made rightly, is formed with flexible exactness. Eliot's "Ash Wednesday" is deliberately religious; however the words of the poem do not come with deep, unimpeded momentum; rather, they arise from a compound of verbal and metrical craftsmanship with a state of personal, religious solicitude. I think it may be said justly that Eliot's work in the last thirty years or so consists of impressive worry adroitly attired.

Every poet of authenticity is simply what he is: Williams is not Whitman. But Williams has this in common with Whitman: It took some time to see that Whitman besides being the rapturous representative man of sky and earth and laborers on the North American continent, was also an artist; and in recent years, Williams, who in 1922 was looked on as a "radical" and somewhat inchoate poet, has been lately seen as cunning and right and artistic with words. Whitman, writing of the poet, by implication chides such persons as T. S. Eliot and Edwin Arlington Robinson: "All beauty," he says, "comes from beautiful blood and a beautiful brain. [The poet's] rhythm and uniformity he will conceal in the roots of his verses, not to be seen of themselves, but to break forth loosely as lilacs in a bush, and take shapes compact as the shapes of melons, or chestnuts, or pears" (*The Poetry and Prose of Walt Whitman*, ed. Untermeyer, p. 534).

What Whitman calls for is met by Williams, not by Eliot. One of the most intense and stirring of Williams' poems is "Portrait of the Author" (this poem I see as more representative of the author than, say, a poem like "The Yachts"). In it Williams is neatly, observantly rhapsodic. Here are some lines:

> Black is split at once into flowers. In
> every bog and ditch, flares of
> small fire, white flowers!—Ah,
> the birches are mad, mad with their green.
> The world is gone, torn into shreds
> with this blessing.

And:

> Take me in your arms, tell me the commonest
> thing that is in your mind to say,
> say anything, I will understand you—![2]

These lines are propulsive; they are like plants swiftly bursting earth and emerging. And surely, poetry can be quieter, seemingly more reluctant. But even in the restraint of Pope and Landor, orderly tumult is to be found.

We look at Eliot again, and take this time some lines from "The Rock":

We thank Thee for the lights that we have kindled,
The light of altar and of sanctuary;
Small lights of those who meditate at midnight
And lights directed through the coloured panes
        of windows
And light reflected from the polished stone.

2. Siegel's earlier discussion of "Portrait of the Author" is on pp. 56-57. See also WCW's comment, p. 105.

I listen to these lines, and look at what visually and otherwise is happening in them. It all seems tame. I remember the radiant, precise urgency of Crashaw and the decorative, honest swoop of Francis Thompson. Crashaw and Thompson are with Williams; for poetry is with Williams. It is poetry as we see it insistently described by—among others—the exploring Coleridge of the *Biographia Literaria* and the thumpingly joyous Hazlitt of the *Lectures on the English Poets* (see the very first page)—whom, by the way, Mr. Eliot has reproved. We need to see that though Coleridge and Hazlitt and Whitman may be added to, they are not superseded in these critical days. They, and the knowing heart of man, are, I think, for Williams; and not, as I understand them, for Eliot.

EDITORS' NOTE. *In late 1966, Thomas De Baggio, editor of the* Washington Independent *(published earlier from Arlington, Virginia, as* Underground*) asked Eli Siegel to review M. L. Rosenthal's The William Carlos Williams Reader. When Mr. Siegel wrote to New Directions requesting a review copy for this purpose, he was told no more were available. Thomas De Baggio obtained a review copy, and Mr. Siegel's review appeared in four parts in the issues of March 22 and April 19, 1967.*

LETTER TO THOMAS DE BAGGIO

Dear Tom De Baggio:

This letter can be taken as a preface to or the first part of my review of *The William Carlos Williams Reader.* In the more formal review I shall send you, consideration of the poetry and prose of Williams will be present. In this letter, preface, or review, I deal with what I call the slyness of M. L. Rosenthal and also the slyness of James Laughlin.

It is true that William Carlos Williams sent many warm, encouraging, laudatory letters to various people. However, there is a certain lack of definitive judgment in these letters. For example, to go to a somewhat different territory, Williams' essay on Marianne Moore can be described as divine and polite rigmarole. I don't think that Williams ever cared for the poetry of Marianne Moore.

Appeared in *Washington Independent*, March 22, 1967.

Consider, in the essay on Marianne Moore, the obviously reluctant eulogy to be found in two sentences like these:

> Miss Moore undertakes in her work to separate poetry from the subject entirely—like all the moderns. In this she has been rarely successful and this is important. (*Williams Reader*, p. 386)[3]

In the more formal part of the review, which may be long, if that seems fitting I shall deal with the phraseology of Williams as found in the Marianne Moore essay and elsewhere.

The fact remains that Williams never wrote a letter like the one he wrote to Martha Baird on November 3, 1951. Any person who compares this letter to the acknowledgments, laudations, social cooings to be found elsewhere, can see a difference.

Furthermore, as you will see, Williams did say to Eli Siegel:

> It's as if everything I've ever done has been for you. You come up with it, and so few people come up with anything. They don't come up with it at all. They praise the wrong things, for the wrong reasons very often, although it seems plain enough; and when you say it, it's plain. You make it plain.[4]

Nothing like this is to be found in any other letter of Williams: where Williams says another person has

3. *The William Carlos Williams Reader*, ed. M. L. Rosenthal (New York: New Directions, 1966).

4. Quoted from *Williams' Poetry Talked about by Eli Siegel, and William Carlos Williams Present and Talking: 1952* (New York: Terrain Gallery, 1964), p. 17.

seen his work squarely. And William Carlos Williams said that Eli Siegel had understood him, with more than thirty people present.

In the Rosenthal anthology, one can see a desire on the part of the sly Mr. Rosenthal to have the Williams letter about Eli Siegel not exist, and to have the book *Hot Afternoons Have Been in Montana: Poems* not exist either. Rosenthal, Laughlin, and others can be as unctuously astonished as they please: the fact remains that they do not want to see a big thing in William Carlos Williams' life as it happened.

In the more formal review, I shall point to an inclination on the part of the adroit Mr. Rosenthal to annul things of poetic meaning when they do not make Mr. Rosenthal comfortable. James Laughlin, like other people, is a votary of his own comfort likewise.

The letter of William Carlos Williams to Martha Baird has in it things that William Carlos Williams says nowhere else. This is as plain as the fact that sunlight and a frying pan are different. When John Thirlwall, in getting up Williams' *Letters,* did not include the November 1951 letter to Martha Baird, he was showing that he belonged to the Rosenthal-Laughlin Evaluation Trend, or what I've elsewhere called the Williams Holding Company.

It is good that James Laughlin reconsidered his first attitude to a review in the *Washington Independent* of a work concerning William Carlos Williams. The reason that he changed is that he saw the opposition to such an attitude as more considerable than he thought.

Meanwhile, in this part of the review, or this letter, I include a quotation from Paul Rosenfeld in his

Port of New York, 1924. This quotation has in it more feeling about Williams' work than is shown these days:

> Curious harmonies of bitter and sweet, of harsh and gentle, of sluggish and swift and sharp and soft in word-color and rhythmical pattern; nude finely viscous little curves of music in which every line is a decisive stroke, render the ironic, contained, humorous dance of the spirit amid the objects of a ramshackle makeshift universe. (*Port of New York*, p. 111)[5]

I shall try to make it clear that M. L. Rosenthal does not see Williams entirely. In the rather short essay that Paul Rosenfeld wrote, he did include the following major lines about tying one's shoelaces:

> My shoes as I lean
> unlacing them[6]

Rosenthal prefers some late stuff that is glazed and unliving compared to this.

Rosenthal doesn't include the great thing about the procedure of a cat:

Poem

> As the cat
> climbed over
> the top of
>
> the jamcloset[7]

5. Paul Rosenfeld, *Port of New York* (New York: Harcourt, Brace, 1924).

Any person who cannot see the difference between large portions of *Paterson,* say, and the naive, musical, methodical astonishment in "Poem" is squinting at the Muses.

The moral of this preface or first part is that everything James Laughlin says doesn't have to be seen as truth uninterrupted. Furthermore, that the literary motives of M. L. Rosenthal don't have to be seen as being as pure as those of St. Francis with the sun or with the birds.

The *Williams Reader* puts the question of what poetry is in still another way, and a way that has to be looked at in our days.

This, then, is the first part of a review. Likewise it is a letter.

Sincerely,
Eli Siegel

---

6. Williams, "The Nightingales," lines 1 and 2. Siegel quoted the whole poem, nine lines, as given by Paul Rosenfeld on page 110 of his book. This version differs from the text in *CEP* (p. 224), where it is in two stanzas of four lines each, the fifth line, "under my feet," being cut.

7. Lines 1-4. The whole poem was quoted. Text is in *CEP,* p. 340. Siegel's earlier discussion of "Poem" is on p. 89 of present volume.

ELI SIEGEL'S REVIEW OF
The William Carlos Williams Reader

I. IS A POET UNDERSTOOD?

Professor M. L. Rosenthal writes a long introduction to the present book; and it must be said that the introduction does not show an understanding of William Carlos Williams, writer and man. It is true that Williams himself did not see himself as well as he would like or as we might like. The fact remains that while Williams—like many poets—did not see himself fully, Mr. Rosenthal as critic doesn't see him either.

It is a pity that with this difficulty of understanding Williams, Professor Rosenthal should make nothing of the fact that Williams did say the present writer had understood his work. The fairly literate people who were there when Williams said this, know that the American poet was not talking hastily or fulsomely or thinly or insincerely. A writer simply felt that he had been understood.

In this review, with its various sections, I shall try, while seeing Williams anew, to show Williams as valuably presenting the problems of poetry, of America, and of a particular self. The questions that Williams had, he respected, though they tormented him; and the answers he gave are truly part of American poetry and of that valuable notation of the world which is literature.

Appeared in *Washington Independent*, March 22 and April 19, 1967.

One has in seeing Williams' poetry the problem of showing where order is present in what looks like casualness, mixup, uninvitingness. Williams wanted to see the uncomely as that in which honesty could find the symmetrical and the classic.

Every poet is a different way of making the free and orderly akin, the careless and the classical friendly. To see where Williams was fond of both the shaped and the askew is to see him as poet.

Williams himself could say incomplete or misleading things on this matter. In a moment of profound exacerbation, he could say what is quoted by Rosenthal in his introduction (page xv):

> There is nothing in literature but change and change is mockery.

It is true that Williams loved change; and it is true that he also hated it. This can be found in the sentence just quoted, for Williams in this rather short sentence says that literature has nothing but change—which seems to be pretty good for change; but then that it is mockery—which seems to be pretty bad. The fact is that Williams loved change and constancy, or the mutable and the everlasting. Poetry does, and Williams was poetic.

In his life we find Williams lingering on the old, what he began with, and looking every day for something he had never seen before. The way Williams' life had in it both a sense of the permanent and an agogness about the new, makes this life good.

I have to say that it is from the top that Professor Rosenthal sees Williams' sense of change and con-

tinuity. In the deepest sense, Rosenthal doesn't have
sympathy for Williams. I feel that were Williams not
established when Rosenthal came to like him, Rosenthal might not have liked him at all. I'm not sure even
now as to the authenticity of Rosenthal's like for the
poetry of Williams. After all, it is possible to write
an introduction to a person's poetry and not like that
poetry. The world is versatile enough to have this
happen.

The Williams question (also torment) is present
likewise in another quotation from the poet Rosenthal
has on the same page as the last (xv):

> It is to the inventive imagination we look for de-
> liverance from every other misfortune as from the
> desolation of a flat Hellenic perfection of style. . . .
> If the inventive imagination must look, as I think,
> to the field of art for its richest discoveries today it
> will best make its way by compass and follow no
> path.

Williams in this passage is saying that aesthetics,
here described as the inventive imagination, is that to
which "we look for deliverance": which means that the
inventive imagination or aesthetics can save the world
if there is any such thing as saving the world. The
nearest thing to God that Williams saw was what he
here calls the inventive imagination. Here he is like
William Blake, for whom, as far as I know, there was
no particular care in Williams.

Williams also has, in the passage quoted, the phrase,
"every other misfortune." A study of Williams' work
makes it clear that Williams saw bad verse, bad economics, bad social relation and bad food as having

something in common. "Every other misfortune," then, is an inclusive term for the world as bad and things in it as bad. Williams could be so hurt by something he saw as unsatisfactory in verse, he could give the appearance of making a judgment, waspishly, on the whole world.

"Hellenic perfection of style," described by Williams as "desolation," is equivalent to that smoothness, that factitious technique, that preference for a shapely box to what might be in the box—which the world has a great deal of. Still, Williams did go after perfection of style. He was as much after rightness of shape, classicality of outline as Horace was or Thomas Stearns Eliot. There are poems of his which are almost geometrical in shape, while what is being said scampers over all the meadows of the world, races down the stairs of the world, bursts out from the boxes of the world, and does havoc with the trim buds of the world.

To instance what I have just said, there is that poem, "The Red Wheelbarrow," which I have been calling a classic these many years.

It is well to look at this poem again. Let us have a classic once more show itself to the folks.

The Red Wheelbarrow

so much depends
upon[8]

Since the present piece is a review of M. L. Rosenthal's *The William Carlos Williams Reader* and Rosenthal's introduction, it is only right that Rosenthal be quoted on the poem. So he is quoted (xvii):

8. The whole poem was quoted. Text is in *CEP*, p. 277. Siegel's earlier discussion of the poem is on pp. 85-89.

The standpoint from which we view that world and its intensities determines the scope of life's meaning for us. The humblest objects of perception are also elements in a symbolic design with a transcendent aesthetic function.

The way Rosenthal takes the meaning of this poem can be described as aloof and professorish. The dear white chickens and the red wheelbarrow are surely given a campus panoply of murky portent. The value of the poem is in the indivisibility of the visual and the philosophic. Williams had an eye, but he was looking for the great burden within what his eye saw, or the value there. Williams was polite most of the time, and he might have nodded approvingly when Rosenthal said that a "standpoint" "determines" a "scope." However, whether Williams would have nodded approvingly or not, I don't see the way Rosenthal expresses himself as being praiseworthy or good English. A standpoint does not determine a scope, either in terms of diction or in terms of what reality offers. And to say that the "humblest objects of perception" are "elements in a symbolic design" is to take away the humility from these humblest objects. The humblest objects are suddenly in an English classroom looking for marks.

The "familiar world," Rosenthal says, is seen "with a fresh eye" in "The Red Wheelbarrow." This is true and true.

What Rosenthal, and others, don't look at is the first line of the poem:

so much depends

Here Williams is overt with his didacticism, with his philosophizing. Williams now is no longer a New Jersey rural citizen with a sharp eye. He takes it upon himself to judge reality; to appraise a possibility of reality.

The line, "so much depends," is one of the vaguest in American literature and also is one of the most freighted.

We can still ask, What is it which depends? while we feel that in being told much depends, we have got something.

Even so it can be asked, what was in Williams' mind when he wrote the three words, "so much depends"?

Rosenthal does not see Williams as philosophic, Williams with a sudden and ever so inclusive judgment of how the world essentially is. Nevertheless, such a judgment is in this poem.

Williams is saying that if a curved useful thing, a wheelbarrow, can be red; and if the red can be glazed with rain water—that is, make a one with something different from red, something not of color; and if the oneness of red wheelbarrow and rain can be attended by living things in white—the white chickens—the diversities of the world, seen boldly, can satisfy human life and a particular mind.

The red wheelbarrow got to something new and larger through being given an amiable, transparent brightness by rain water—and a wheelbarrow and rain water are so different! The wheelbarrow's habitation is a yard, while rain water comes from anonymous loftiness. But look! we have something of another world in the white of those white, domestic chickens. The fact that chickens can have the color of holiness and still be fussy creatures, is their affirmation of there being a tremendous friendship between the red of a wheelbarrow and the colorless wetness of water fallen from above.

The case is clear, the writer says: the jangle of the data of the world is pleasing music when the jangle is truly heard. Poetry has been saying something like this for a long while, but the specific objects in this poem were got together first by Williams.

And then Williams, while his eye was busy, came to a musical way of telling what his eye saw.

"So much depends" is simply two iambics, but it seems to cover a great deal even while it is below something, hangs from it.

The word "upon," the second line, is swift and sharp, almost like the most successful peck of one of those white chickens.

We have a space then, a space between a preposition and the noun to which it belongs. The third line consists of the brightest color in the world, given a home in one iambic, "a red." And the third line consists too of a word, "wheel," which in its going on, is different from the still stoppage in the sound of "a red."

"Barrow" is the fourth line and is a study in the power of the magnificent consonant *b* along with two heavy vowels, *a* and *ow*, separated by two growling and functional *r*'s. The world growls as we are prepared for rain to glaze the object the growling is concerned with: barrow.

A construction somewhat the reverse of the first line is in the fifth line, "glazed with rain." "So much" rises, while "glazed" is content in smooth flatness. "With rain" is an iambic like "depends," but instead of having

the logical vagueness of "depends," has a something
that place and life show often: rain.

"Water," the sixth line, has a stillness which can
dramatically be placed against the protesting quality
of "barrow."

While these prosodic and perceptual things are going
on, rain is making ontological love to a red wheelbarrow.

In the last two lines, we have a surprise. One would
think that the white chickens would be beside the red
wheelbarrow. It isn't that way, though. The red wheelbarrow is beside the white chickens. This means that a
circle, the wheel, keeps company with moving, warm,
but holy objects: the white chickens. "Beside the
white" as meter is pretty much like "so much depends."
But while "so much depends" is matter of fact and
philosophic, "beside the white," with the two deep *i*
sounds, screams indignity.

And the poem ends with the word "chickens," fraught
with domesticity, liveliness, and the mystery of the
yard.

Well, that is about "The Red Wheelbarrow," which
is one of the true Williams poems.

M. L. Rosenthal, however, like others, does not see
the quality of the early poems. There is a tendency too
much on the part of Rosenthal to make an unsuccessful
poem like "The Yachts," or "Asphodel, That Greeny
Flower" of similar value to "Postlude," "Metric Figure,"
"Dawn," "The Nightingales."

So much of Williams' good work is left out for the
inferior one could cry.

I suppose one can see from this first section of a
review that I don't belong to the Rosenthal set. Later

in this fairly long review, I shall give evidence pointing not only to Rosenthal's not being of my set but to his wish that I hadn't said anything about Williams at all, and to his wish that Williams had said nothing about me or to me. At this point it is well to say that what poetry is, is the chief thing; and that what Williams is as poet is inseparable from this chief thing.

II. WILLIAMS IN PERSPECTIVE

It is by now clear that Williams belongs with the American poets of all time: which means that he is with such persons as Poe, Emerson, Dickinson, Whitman, Hart Crane, Stevens, Lindsay, and others. It may be said also that he is with William Cullen Bryant, so different from him in technique, and yet alike; for Bryant went into the being of a waterfowl going South somewhat as Williams got himself into the being of an outraged sparrow. However all this may be, it would be proper to see the work of Williams next to one of those American poets whom years ago Houghton Mifflin included among the Cambridge Poets; and the chances are, Williams would have more poetry.

The fact is that Williams was poetic often enough to have a body of poetry appropriately entitled Works— by this is meant poetic works. To work at poetry and do a good job often, is not the characteristic thing in the land between the Atlantic and Pacific and north of the Gulf and south of the Lakes. And that Williams has a work called *The William Carlos Williams Reader* is a sign that he belongs with something like the ages, with the classic, with the tested.

Since Williams is with the American poets and with the poets generally, it is well that his distinguishing quality be ascertained and lingered on. I do not think that Professor Rosenthal has seen what this distinguishing quality is, liked it, and affirmed it.

To illustrate my demur at the taste of Rosenthal, I quote a real Williams poem, a poem of the Williams that wasn't yet sanctified, flattened, and taken for somebody else by the poetic trend-watchers. The poem is "The Nightingales":

> My shoes as I lean
> unlacing them[9]

It happens that neither Emerson nor Poe, neither Whitman nor Dickinson, neither Millay nor Lindsay— and for that matter, neither Stevens nor Hart Crane— was inclined or were inclined to make so much of unlacing shoes. In this poem, we have Williams sharply looking for the absolute, the eternal, and the surprising in an ordinary operation: one that has humility in it and necessity. That Williams should have seen the shadows of his fingers to be like nightingales is also an instance of the Williams response to the absolute become particular.

"The Nightingales" is not included by Professor Rosenthal. Apparently he thinks "The Yachts" is a better poem and that "Asphodel, That Greeny Flower" is a better poem. It should be said, and I say it right now, that neither "The Yachts" nor "Asphodel, That Greeny Flower"—though admittedly written by Wil-

---

9. The whole poem was quoted. Text is in *CEP*, p. 224.

liams—is deeply Williams at all. These poems lack that subterraneously triumphant sharpness that is Williams' most felicitous endowment. "The Yachts" is structurally impressive and "Asphodel, That Greeny Flower" has a bravura symmetry in triplets; but they both have a languid width, sprawl unintensely, and mark time poetically. The asphodel poem is ever so affecting from the point of view of life itself, but as a poem it is not true to Williams.

The chief thing differentiating a poem like "The Nightingales" from a poem like "Asphodel" is what makes the poetic line the poetic line. Williams pondered on the nature of the line as much as he did about anything; he can be said to have worshipped the line as much as he worshipped anything.

There is a difference, in terms of the line, between

The sexual orchid that bloomed then

of "Asphodel," and

Nimbly the shadows

or

flat worsted flowers

of "The Nightingales." There is a vowel and consonant drama and a world-as-seen drama in the lines just quoted, which are not present in "Asphodel," in much of *Paterson,* and in "The Yachts" of Williams.

A deep unconscious purpose of Williams was to make the sharp and cutting, wide and gentle. He wanted to find the everlasting in the staccato.

It is this musical nimbleness that Williams had and has which distinguishes him from his fellow poets in American literature. The scratch, the scrape, the sudden turn, the angle unlooked for—made musical— were the world made plain and likable and honest to Williams.

I think it is just because Poe is so different in his metrical effects and in the way he wanted to find an undying symmetry in the world, that made Williams eulogize him so inaccurately in *In the American Grain*.

When the history of poetry is written, it will be found that there is something in common among Alexander Pope, Percy Bysshe Shelley, Matthew Arnold, William Butler Yeats, Algernon Charles Swinburne, and William Carlos Williams—and among William Carlos Williams and many others. The thing in common between Williams and other poets is that they cared for reality as distinct individuals and that the distinct way that they cared for the world was impelled to be musical.

William Carlos Williams showed that the short free verse line could be musical. He succeeded where his friend Ezra Pound generally failed. The short free verse line can have an unmistakable and deep music —but this music doesn't grow on every blackberry bush, nor does it jingle from every round plate.

It must be said that in the field of prose, Williams is not as important as he is in the field of the poetic line.

Kora in Hell looks like prose, but the best things in it could be broken up into short lines with poetry ensuing. It happens that I told Williams that his *Kora in Hell*, which in March 1952 he had forgotten, was more important than he thought. He seems to have agreed with this later, as others did.

When one looks at the selections from *The Great American Novel* given in the *Williams Reader*, the one thing that takes over is disappointment. Williams had a way of maundering, hoping that something would happen. He shows his capacity for fumbling with the unwilling locks of his unconscious in *The Great American Novel*. Perhaps nothing that's real is dispensable, but if anything is dispensable, *The Great American Novel* asks to be considered.

A Voyage to Pagany has prose of sharp account in it. Strictly as a novel, though, it doesn't much matter. Jane Austen couldn't write "The Widow's Lament in Springtime" (fortunately included in the *Williams Reader*), but Williams couldn't construct a novel the way *Pride and Prejudice* is constructed. The English spinster could just do something the Rutherford doctor couldn't.

Williams' short stories are better, but you miss the touch of Hawthorne, Maupassant, and even O. Henry. Eudora Welty and Hortense Calisher know things about the short story that Williams didn't. I'm talking now of the short story *as* short story. There is writing about a mother and son in one of Williams' short stories which can't be left out when the more distasteful and frightening aspects of the family are considered by some judicious historian. A scene, though, is not the same as a short story, which is that and all that.

And how far Eudora Welty and Hortense Calisher are from being able to write one of those mischievous, musical poems in which the universe comes to be present through a few scratches and twirls!

In the matter of American history, Williams is uncertain. There's no doubt that Williams was affected by the history of America as a matter of geography, time, and a person or persons. He shows, however, a tendency to do that which is just contrary to what a doctor does as he looks through a microscope. Williams is like D. H. Lawrence in a tendency to look at the nearest hill and run up that hill, even though the hill is not exactly the subject. Williams and Lawrence also had a tendency to run impressively down neighboring declivities, though these declivities were not the most relevant things either. If one asks, while reading *In the American Grain*: Just what is being got at?—the question is neither insensitive nor unkind.

Suppose we take a paragraph from the essay on Edgar Allan Poe. It is one of those paragraphs in which someone seems to say everything. Lawrence could give the appearance of saying everything—at least the ineffable—and Williams could give that appearance too. With all my care for Williams, I have to say that the paragraph I now quote is a fraud:

> One is forced on the conception of the New World as a woman. Poe was a new De Soto. The rest might be content with little things, not he. (*Williams Reader*, p. 363)

Poe was not a new De Soto, and the concept of the New World as a woman does not force itself on one. It was simply a day for Williams in which De Soto and Poe had to be together. Later in the essay, Poe is given "the identical gesture of a Boone" (p. 368). All this means is that Williams liked Poe and he also liked Boone, and he felt he had to show it.

Like other poets, Williams was not sure of himself as a critic. The essay on Marianne Moore, reprinted in the *Reader*, shows this. Williams often felt he should be stirred and therefore changed a situation in which no stir was present into one in which stir was present.

Williams, like humanity itself, had energy and languor, drive and disinclination. His *Autobiography* shows this. Cellini and Rousseau seem much more interested in their lives than Williams is. And you don't have to go to Cellini or Rousseau. There is a slowness in the *Autobiography* which manifested the Williams of the time he wrote it. Many facts are there, but they are listlessly given.

The great fact about William Carlos Williams is that frequently he changed the honesty which he as himself had into a poetic music different from previous poetic music. That music is present in the poem which once took Paul Rosenfeld:

Poem

As the cat
climbed over
the top of

the jamcloset[10]

The *Williams Reader* puts Williams squarely in American poetry. I was once told by Williams that I understood his work. He told me this with an honest

10. The whole poem was quoted. Siegel's earlier discussion of "Poem" is on p. 89.

pomp and with quite a few people listening. Whether I understand Williams' work or not, it should be understood. In understanding Williams, I think we shall have to be somewhat different from M. L. Rosenthal, editor of the *Williams Reader*.

FIRST THOUGHTS ON
THE WILLIAMS HOLDING COMPANY

When a poet definitely emerges from the many and is seen as nationally important, there come to be a number of people about him who act like a family and also like a holding company. When you give your praise to a poet and you think about him, and more than that, you have met him—you come to believe that this poet belongs to you in a way that he does not belong to the unchosen—and the unchosen is a synonym for everyone else.

There is the Williams Holding Company, some of the members of which I know and have endured things from, and some of whom I don't know. When you think you possess a person, whether in love or literature, the unjust may take place, but what is interesting, too: for the unjust is often interesting.

The first sight of the Williams Holding Company, dim though it was, was when Dr. Williams, after having said, with great sincerity, he wanted to hear of how Aesthetic Realism looked on *Hamlet*, failed to come, without telling that he was unable to.

What appears happened was that William Carlos Williams was told he had gone too far in praising Eli Siegel and in seeing Eli Siegel as mattering in his life. Did it seem the best thing to do, one could find out who these friends were who cautioned Dr. Williams against Eli Siegel. There was a Williams Holding Company in 1952. And it should be said that it was in

Appeared in *Washington Independent*, April 19, 1967.

January 1952 that I, from one point of view, joined the holding company by meeting him and talking to him for a fairly long time. Had I conformed, I have no doubt I would not only be a member of the holding company from the technical point of view, but from the deep, unctuous point of view.

As the holding company was operating, the letter that William Carlos Williams wrote to Martha Baird remained. Also what Williams said with about thirty-five people present, was recorded; and that remained. In all factuality it has to be said that the expressions William Carlos Williams used in writing (the Baird letter) and in talking, were most unusual. However unusual they were, they were deeply authentic and were used by him without any previous coaxing whatsoever, or social pressure.

I am afraid that the holding company did not like this. Indeed, I have no doubt that the holding company did not like this.

I do not know whether Judson Jerome of the *Antioch Review* is a working and orthodox member of the holding company. But Mr. Jerome acted like one when he reviewed *Hot Afternoons* in the *Antioch Review*. Jerome did not inquire; he just went ahead, and in the *Antioch Review* dealt with the Williams letter to Martha Baird as if it were a hoax. This was effrontery of a profound and noxious kind. But if you are a member of the holding company or if you have, without being a member, its spirit, you can do such things.

It may be said at this point that the letter of William Carlos Williams to Martha Baird is now in a safety vault, and if a question arises as to its authenticity, that authenticity can be ascertained. People have felt that the Williams letter was genuine—who knew Williams, and were not in the holding company—because it sounded like Williams. It is the Williams prose as we find it elsewhere, only saying something that was different from what he said elsewhere.

So there have been a few sentences for Judson Jerome.

And then there is John Thirlwall. Professor Thirlwall edited a book of Williams' letters and left the Williams letter to Baird out. He knew that it existed; in fact, he had a copy of it. It is quite clear that if the Williams letter is genuine, it represents an important point in his life, and shows a large and most infrequent emotion.

I say in all sincerity, the Williams enthusiasm in the Baird letter is a big thing in the life of Williams and a big thing within the possibility of literary emotion, or of poetic judgment.

Why did Professor Thirlwall fail to include this letter? Was it because he felt it was unimportant? I do not think so. I think Professor Thirlwall chose to act as if the letter were not real. To the holding company, the letter could not seem real.

The holding company affected Williams himself. It or they made it seem that a large feeling of some concern to American literature was an aberration, a will-o'-the-wisp, a moment of frantic misjudgment. Uncertainty can exist in a person's mind, and it existed in Williams'; but the holding company encouraged the less handsome uncertainties.

I do not know of all the operations of the holding company. I know that Michael Weaver, of Cambridge and of Yale, working through a grant on American poetry, showed for a while a deep interest in the

Williams that had written to Martha Baird and had talked to me, and of whom I talked. How I talked of Williams with Williams listening is now in a publication called *Williams' Poetry Talked about by Eli Siegel, and William Carlos Williams Present and Talking: 1952*.

I am afraid that Michael Weaver of England was affected by the holding company or its spirit. This is sad.

The latest clear manifestation of the holding company's outlook was shown by James Laughlin of New Directions. I was asked by Tom De Baggio of the *Washington Independent* to review the *Williams Reader*, and I wrote a note to New Directions asking that a copy be sent to me. A postcard came from New Directions, rather belatedly, saying that reviewers' copies had been exhausted. I am afraid that reviewers' copies were exhausted because Mr. Laughlin is a member of the holding company and acts in keeping with its purpose, its possessiveness, and its prejudice.

Well, there is the Williams Holding Company, a sketch of which has been given here. Like other possessive groups, domestic or cultural or both, it does not serve the best interests of the human mind or of men and women.

And the Williams letter to Martha Baird of November 3, 1951, is authentic. It still serves as an introduction to *Hot Afternoons Have Been in Montana: Poems*, because it belongs there.

5

Afterword
by Ellen Reiss

Part Five

The relationship of William Carlos Williams and Eli Siegel is important in literary history. How important becomes clearer when we look at statements in Williams' essays and letters about the writers of his time.

Williams was famous for encouraging new poets. Karl Shapiro tells of sending his first book of poems, when he was twenty, to several famous poets, and the only one who even answered was Williams. Shapiro says, "Williams did not praise my book, but his letter . . . was full of sympathy and kindliness for a young man who wanted to be a poet."[1]

Williams wrote so many introductions, there was a time when another introduction by WCW didn't carry much weight. However, while he was lavish in lending his name, it has not been so well seen that, as with Shapiro, Williams was exceedingly chary of his praise.

His introduction to Allen Ginsberg's *Howl* in 1956 is one of the most celebrated. Looking at it, what do

1. Karl Shapiro, *In Defense of Ignorance* (New York: Random House, 1960), p. 143. Shapiro makes indirect reference to Williams' letter about Siegel: "Siegel's 'Hot Afternoons'—which Williams alone had the courage and honesty to reintroduce" (p. 150), giving both the author's name and the title of the poem incompletely. Shapiro does not deal with the letter as a serious and important expression of Williams, though much of his chapter on Williams is about Williams as critic.

we find? It is four paragraphs long—a page and a half. It is chiefly about Allen Ginsberg's life. There is admiration for his ability to survive, wonder at what he has been through. As to what is actually said about Ginsberg's poetry, there are two unequivocal, clear phrases: "an arresting poem" and "a well-made poem."[2]

Poetically, Williams was not easily pleased. This holds true not only for the younger, less known poets but for those generally regarded as his peers. Search his recorded comments: you will find nothing that compares with the 1951 letter about Siegel in prolonged lucidity, in intense and unequivocal resoundingness of praise.

In a letter to Kay Boyle of 1932, Williams gave his opinion of the chief poets of the century:

> Let us once and for all understand that Eliot is finally and definitely dead. . . . Ezra Pound is too "like" the classics. . . . Jeffers has not been able to overcome poetic diction. . . . Robinson? Well, if you can find anything there. To me it seems stiff English. . . . Wallace Stevens has something more than his play with sequences of sound. . . . Worth reading again. . . . The bucolic simplicity of Robert Frost seems to me a halt. The English writers I exclude axiomatically.[3]

Here, Stevens is praised most: "worth reading again" —but it is hardly encomiastic.

2. Allen Ginsberg, *Howl and Other Poems* (San Francisco: City Lights Books, 1956), p. 8.

3. *The Selected Letters of William Carlos Williams*, ed. John C. Thirlwall (New York: McDowell, Obolensky, 1957), pp. 129-132.

In a later letter: "Auden's lines are dead—tho thoughtful."[4]

And there is this bit of negativism on Joyce: "His island choked him in the end, made him clutch his throat, out of which the garbled speech flowed."[5]

In March 1947 he wrote to Robert McAlmon about a book by Edith Sitwell. He likes her more than most, but he sounds irritated: "Firm, convincing poetry. Very wonderful. 'Green something or other,' I've forgot the name of the book. Did you ever meet the woman?"[6]

The closest thing in Williams' correspondence to unqualified praise of another poet is about Carl Sandburg. For this, we have to go all the way back to 1917. In a letter to Harriet Monroe, Williams said:

> Sandburg's "In the Cool Tombs" is a splendid thing. I hope with all my power to hope that I may meet Sandburg soon. He is, if I am not mistaken, really studying his form. . . . Sandburg is really thinking like an artist.[7]

Williams wavered about Sandburg later, and even here he speaks of Sandburg as "studying form," making progress. What he says of Siegel is in an altogether different key:

> I am thrilled. . . . We are not up to Siegel, even yet. . . . That single poem, out of a thousand others written in the past quarter century, secures our

4. *Selected Letters*, p. 264.
5. *Selected Letters*, p. 237.
6. *Selected Letters*, p. 256.
7. *Selected Letters*, p. 41.

place in the cultural world. I make such a statement only after a lifetime of thought and experience, I make it deliberately. . . . We are obliged to follow what Siegel instinctively set down. We are compelled to pursue his lead. . . . This is powerful evidence of a new track. . . . the truly new. . . . The sheer inability of the general mind to grasp what has taken place. . . . But at last I am just beginning to know, to know firmly what the present day mind is seeking.

Had the 1951 letter to Martha Baird been included among Williams' *Selected Letters*, which it was not, a reader coming upon it would have felt something immediately different, revolutionary.

Yet, not only did Thirlwall omit this letter from his collection, but no subsequent writer on Williams has given it serious attention, nor even mentioned it in such a way as to give readers an idea of its real tone and content.

Linda Wagner in *The Poems of William Carlos Williams* ignores the letter, though her book is filled with quotations from Williams' correspondence, published and unpublished. James Guimond in *The Art of William Carlos Williams* quotes passages from it with ellipses and paraphrases so it appears that what Williams said about Siegel he is really saying about himself.[8] Emily Mitchell Wallace's *A Bibliography of William Carlos Williams* (sumptuous in its bibliographical descriptions, noticing even spacing errors in printing) asserts, "Dated November 3, 1951, the letter thanks

8. James Guimond, *The Art of William Carlos Williams* (Urbana: University of Illinois Press, 1968), p. 187.

Martha Baird for a copy of Eli Siegel's 'Hot Afternoons Have Been in Montana.' "⁹ Clearly, Mrs. Wallace's description lessens the letter's importance.

The *Selected Letters* show that Dr. Williams, like
most people, did not feel he had been seen fairly in
his life. The closest he comes to saying anyone saw his
work accurately is in a letter of 1934 to Marianne
Moore:

> The thing that I like best about your review of my
> book is that you have looked at what I have done
> through my own eyes. . . . Had it not been so you
> would not have noticed the "inner security" nor the
> significance of some of the detail—which nobody
> seems to value as I have valued it.¹⁰

Williams does not say that a direction in his whole
work has been shown to him. He praises Miss Moore
by affirming that she saw what he did; but he does
not suggest that she saw what he could not see himself. And he does not imply that she has anything large
to teach him.

What Williams heard the evening of March 5, 1952
was different from anything he had heard about his
work, in a period of about forty years, and from some
of the most brilliant people in America. One can look
at reviews and essays by Ezra Pound, Wallace Stevens,
Yvor Winters, Marianne Moore, Robert Lowell, which

9. Emily Mitchell Wallace, *A Bibliography of William Carlos
Williams* (Middletown, Conn.: Wesleyan University Press,
1968), p. 230.
10. *Selected Letters,* p. 147.

vary in depth and keenness, and ask about any one of them: Did this make Dr. Williams feel someone knew him?

In the discussion after Siegel's talk, he speaks as if he is finally finding the answers he has wanted. He asks about death, and about God:

> WILLIAMS. I notice when you talk about "God or," you say something of that sort. What is the—
> SIEGEL. God is the thing that connects objects. That's what you're writing about.

Williams was skeptical of philosophy. But what he was affected by was Aesthetic Realism—the idea that, literally, "the world, art, and self explain each other: each is the aesthetic oneness of opposites." This way of seeing the world was in Siegel's poetry, making Williams write, "We are compelled to pursue his lead." And it was in what Siegel said on March 5, which caused Williams to reply:

> It's as if everything I've ever done has been for you. . . . You make it plain. And it's very forceful. . . . It really is beyond what I see.

And then there ensued what is likely the most significant silence in literary history.

II

The response of Williams to Siegel has a likeness to that of other people who have been affected by him. No one has been met with such extremes of admiration and insult, love and coldness as Siegel, and perhaps we do not yet have the perspective to understand that disparity fully.

Dr. Williams was the literary person who reacted most generously and honestly to Siegel's work; yet in him too the insult and the coldness were present, with a discrepancy that was tremendous. I should like to say something of what I have seen for myself, for the purpose of having the change in Williams better comprehended.

At the time the principal occurrences of this documentary took place, I was seven years old. I sometimes attended Aesthetic Realism lessons with my parents, who were present at Siegel's talk on the poetry of Williams. In January 1952, my parents and I had a lesson in which Mr. Siegel spoke to me about music. According to my mother's notes, he asked me this:

> Do you want to be like music? If people know how to conduct themselves they can be like music. Melody can teach you how to rise and fall and see that you are the same person. According to Aesthetic Realism, the things that make for beauty not only in music but in pictures and writing and talking are the things that people want. Is there a music in words too?

In those early lessons my self was described, as I felt it to be, inside. And meanwhile the whole world was present. I was being educated in what Williams called "the poem as a way of life."

My impression of Mr. Siegel then is coherent with my present opinion of him, and as far as I have seen, with the opinion of everyone who has heard him speak.

Eli Siegel is a human being, our contemporary, with as vast an amount of knowledge as any person in the history of the world. When you hear him speak, you know you are listening to someone great, greater than anyone you have ever seen. Yet Siegel is not great in some majestic way, though he has majesty. He can talk about a particular thing—a syllable of a word, or an event in history, or your anger at 3 P.M.—with a precision that makes you see *it*. I have seen nowhere but in Siegel an ease about the whole universe, about every subject, every person, that comes from respect for it. Ease and reverence are in his poems. That is what made Williams say Siegel "got to an absolutely unspoiled point of practice." It makes him able to be humorous without contempt, as most people cannot be, and able to show anger with an exactitude and mightiness one finds principally in art.

Siegel's logic is unremitting, and it is not cold: I think he has had the most beautiful emotions, and the largest, of any person in the world, and that he is the person in history most unafraid to know himself. I have never seen him unkind or petty. There is kindness even when he is most critical; and this can make one ashamed of one's own selfishness, and angry, even while it is the thing one has hoped most to find.

In a certain way, Siegel is the most ordinary person I have met. He is not ostentatious. There is a simplicity of honesty about him. He is a person whose desire to know is greater than anything else—and this makes him both humble and magnificent.

Eli Siegel is the person I love most in the world. Ever so many others feel this. All that is true about his character is in his writings: his poetry, his criticism, his philosophic work. It is communicable and permanent.

Yet I must say that even in 1952 I was not just pleased by my opinion of Siegel. And my displeasure at an early age and later has a likeness to the displeasure of others, including Dr. Williams. I saw very early that there was a large difference between Siegel and the other persons I knew. Others I had met, parents and teachers, were good in some things; but then there were areas where they were selfish or hypocritical, and therefore I could limit my respect for them and feel superior when I wanted. I could not do this with Siegel, though I tried. There is an exchange of contempt that goes on among people: I can fool you and will let you fool me when convenient. Siegel won't make that exchange.

I have hoped that someone would find the flaw in Siegel's thought I couldn't find, or show that he really took all he knows from Hegel or Kant or some obscure philosopher. The very scope of Siegel's knowledge, which was making it possible for me to see in a way I could be proud of, also angered me.

There is evidence that Williams too did not just welcome Siegel's largeness. In the letter to Martha Baird he is "thrilled" by it, and meets Siegel's grandeur with grandeur of his own: "He has outstripped the world of his time. . . . Everything we most are compelled to do is in that one poem." Yet as the communication ends, there is a falling off, a grudgingness: "What I can do to be of practical assistance to you in pushing Siegel's work, so monumentally neglected, I don't know. . . . I can't give much time." He does not want to read Siegel's lecture on technique, would "rather see ES write than reason about writing."

When Williams heard Siegel speak, and realized that the seeing in his poems had been continuous, that, as Martha Baird said, Siegel "is an artist all the time," he was amazed. He said on March 5, "I am astonished. I value your words." But in a letter three days later he called it, dismissingly, "just talk."

It is hard to respond justly to greatness, when it is current and concerns one's own life. And Siegel's unprecedented lack of recognition, which Williams describes in his letter, makes largeness of mind a thousand times more difficult. Yet Williams is distinguished in this matter: much, at least, of his response was beautiful.

As a child I could not make sense of this discrepancy: what I was learning in Aesthetic Realism classes was very important; yet Aesthetic Realism was not taught in school, Siegel was not on television, other people had not heard of him, and when I spoke they made me feel my opinion was peculiar. I soon learned either not to talk about Siegel at all, or to speak in a casual way and hide the respect I felt. I did this for a long time. It is what Williams did.

Williams heard from his literary friends the kind of talk about Siegel anyone can hear. I have listened to it in abundance, all through college and graduate school, from fellow-students and professors who wanted to "take care" of me. The attempt is to show that Siegel is a publicity seeker and wants to use one to get ahead. He wrote a poem in 1925 and has been capitalizing on it ever since. He has a forceful personality, by which he has adroitly gathered a body of naive and zealous devotees—but his thought is really watered-down Hegel, or Coleridge, or Lao-tzu, or Heraclitus, or Aristotle. I have even been told it was watered-down Wallace Stevens.

My master's and doctor's theses are written from the point of view of Aesthetic Realism, and in both cases I had to work hard to convince advisors and committees to let me use it. I was told that my ideas were fine—but couldn't I keep the approach and just not mention Siegel?

I have been talked to this way: "Are you still involved with Siegel?"; "Are you his latest protégé?"; "Don't hitch your wagon to Siegel's star"; "He's not an accepted scholar"; "We don't want you to become narrow and ruin your mind"; and worse. But I never was asked, "What is your opinion of Siegel, and why?" "Cultured" people, like other people, do not want to learn anything large from someone without sufficient prestige to make them feel important.

Williams had heard plenty of gossip before he wrote to Martha Baird about Siegel's poems in 1951, and he may not have been too anxious to say to his literary friends what he says to her. The absence of Gascoyne, Frankenberg, Untermeyer, Vivienne Koch, and Mrs. Williams from Siegel's lecture shows where Williams' friends stood. When Williams did attempt to say what he felt, he must have met what I and others have met: flattering disapproval from friends who wanted to "protect" him: "Oh, you don't want to get involved with that," accompanied by a wave of the hand; and gossip of the crudest sort served up pleasantly by educated people over a cup of coffee or a drink.

One can imagine what this did to Williams. I know what it has done to me. I have been on university campuses and known that the people I thought were important wanted me to act as if my largest emotions did not exist, as if my best insights came from a source other than their true one. And because I was not comfortable with the size of my respect, I often complied.

The thing I am most proud of in my life is having seen the value of Siegel's thought and work. Williams' letter, and the way he talked afterward, show he was proud of this too. Yet, in an academic milieu, I have felt my proudest perceptions grow somewhat hazy— as if something I greatly prized were slipping through my fingers, and I wanted it to. I was ashamed, and angry with Siegel because I was ashamed. The Museum of Modern Art reading, with its tepidity and aloofness, indicates to me that Williams did what I did. The accounts of the telephone conversation and the letters in the winter of 1952 show Williams was afraid to see Siegel, even though he wanted to very much. I sometimes used to want to stay away from Siegel's classes because I knew I would see and feel something large I was not prepared to take care of. It is possible to wish what you are most grateful for never occurred.

III

Professor Thirlwall includes in the *Selected Letters* one Williams wrote to Robert Lowell on March 11, 1952, just six days after he had told Siegel, "It's as if everything I've ever done has been for you." The letter is rather sickening.

Williams writes to Lowell nothing of having met Siegel or heard anything from him (Siegel is, in fact, mentioned in none of the *Selected Letters*), and nothing of his opinion of "Hot Afternoons." Instead he asserts, "I've become interested in a young poet, Allen Ginsberg"; and speaks about what he could have learned about the line from T. S. Eliot: "Eliot could have saved me many years with that had he been willing to remain here and put his weight behind the working of the thing out. . . . Both Pound and Eliot have been faithful artists, both have refused to weaken."[11]

Throughout his career Williams had disliked and distrusted Eliot; and on March 5, Siegel confirmed the dislike and showed the aesthetic justice of it. Now, suddenly, Williams tells Lowell that a letter of Lowell's "has changed my attitude toward Eliot more than anything I have ever read of him. I accept him now for what he is, I have never been willing before to do that." And it is Eliot who could teach Williams about the line![12]

Williams had said he had been unable to write a poem for years. On March 5 he told Siegel, "You've opened up a lot of new territory for me." Six days later he writes to Lowell, "Maybe there'll be a 5th book

---

11. *Selected Letters*, pp. 312, 313. All references to the Lowell letter are to these pages.

12. Karl Shapiro comments on Williams' sudden change about Eliot in this letter to Lowell: "he seemed about to revise his opinion of Eliot." Shapiro could not know the real point of reference is Siegel, who is not mentioned, and attributes Williams' change to "personal loyalty" and "an overpowering desire to be fair." See *In Defense of Ignorance*, p. 146.

of *Paterson.*" He does not tell Lowell what he really saw.

It is easier to say, "I wish I could go to Ischia next year. Auden offered me or us his villa there, but I did not take him up." The villa of Auden, whom Williams did not respect, was more in keeping with what he felt to be his life and position than the lecture of Siegel, whose meaning he saw as so large. No wonder Williams behaved as he did at the Museum reading two weeks later. No wonder he did not come to hear Siegel lecture on *Hamlet.*

Following the one to Lowell in the *Selected Letters* are two letters to David McDowell, dated May 5, 1952 and June 24, 1952. Williams has been ill, and writes, "Some days during the last three weeks (for some unknown reason) I felt as if I was about to cash in my chips. . . . God knows you need your friends. I need mine, all of them."[13]

As Williams grows more cool to Siegel, he grows depressed, fears another cerebral hemorrhage. We can ask whether it is possible that the last years of Williams' life would have been different had Williams acted more in keeping with what he really felt.

In January 1955, Williams composed for John Thirlwall a letter, rather famous, in which he describes the need for a "new measure" in poetry. It is eminently unclear, and the lack of clarity may be partly the result of Dr. Williams' desire to change what he had seen. He asserts to Thirlwall:

> It is part of our present situation in the world that when we perceive an alternative to our actions

13. *Selected Letters,* pp. 313-314.

which enlarges the field which they occupy, we feel
inevitably impelled to give them the head to go
where they are called. . . . There are leads . . .
which point the way to approaching changes.[14]

Williams had written to Martha Baird of Eli Siegel
three years earlier that he

has outstripped the world of his time in several very
important respects. Technical respects. . . . We are
compelled to pursue his lead. Everything we most
are compelled to do is in that one poem.

Williams found what he thought "the present day mind
is seeking." But now he tells Thirlwall that the last
innovation in poetic technique was Whitman's, and
goes on in this muddled way about an alternative to
actions, which enlarges their field, and also calls them,
so that we give actions "the head to go."

As the letter goes on, Williams makes a relation of
poetry and physics, and one may ask, Was he thinking of what Siegel had said in March 1952 relating the
poetic line to the quantum theory? Williams had not
made such a comparison before that:

But when availability for human expression is
broached, the structure of the poetic line itself
enters the field. That is where aesthetics is mated
with physics.

This letter to Thirlwall is meant as Williams' artic-
ulation of the "new" he was searching for within the

14. *Selected Letters,* p. 330. All references to the Thirlwall
letter are to this page and the page that follows.

technique of a poem, which would change men's lives. It shares with the letter to Martha Baird and other letters a certain similarity of phraseology and ideas. Compare, for instance, these two statements, the first to Thirlwall, the second to Martha Baird:

> So what can we do but retreat to some "standard" which we have known in the past and say to ourselves, Beyond this standard you shall not go!

> Almost everyone wants to run back to the old practices. You can't blame him. He wants assurance, security, . . . approval.

Throughout his life Williams was looking for the "new" and for a way of seeing that was beautiful. And, as the sentences just quoted show, he was afraid of the thing in himself that could want not to honor it.

In 1951 Williams found this "new" in the poetry of Eli Siegel and said so in his letter, and the March 1952 lecture confirmed what he had seen. After that, Williams spent his time trying to cover up what had happened, even as he tried to use what he had learned.

The late, long poem "Asphodel, That Greeny Flower," published the year of the letter to Thirlwall, has been called a "love poem" to his wife, Flossie. But "Asphodel" has more torment and guilt than love. And it has these important lines at the end of Book I:

> Look at
> what passes for the new.
> You will not find it there but in
> despised poems.
> It is difficult

to get the news from poems
                    yet men die miserably every day
                              for lack
of what is found there.
                    Hear me out
                              for I too am concerned
and every man
                    who wants to die at peace in his bed
                              besides.[15]

I know of no place where Williams talks so strik-
ingly of poems being "despised" as in his description
of the way Siegel was treated: "Even I," he wrote, "was
not up to a full realization of what the *Narr*, the 'fool,'
Siegel had done." If we take the "despised poems" to
be Siegel's poems, the lines follow powerfully. Men die
miserably every day for lack of what is in these poems
—which Williams had said in 1951 showed him what
"the present day mind is seeking." And to make sure
the general "men" is understood to include himself, he
expostulates: "Hear me out"—which has the ring of
an old argument—and then says plainly, "for I too am
concerned." So much so that it concerned his dying at
peace.

IV

Many besides Williams, in meeting Eli Siegel and his
thought, have seen it as necessary to praise and then
be silent. Mark Van Doren, Joseph Wood Krutch,

15. "Asphodel, That Greeny Flower," *Pictures from Brueghel
and Other Poems* (New York: New Directions, 1967), pp. 161-
162.

and Lewis Gannett were the judges who awarded Siegel the *Nation* poetry prize in 1925 for "Hot Afternoons Have Been in Montana." After the poem was printed and its twenty-two-year-old author was the center of a storm of controversy, not one of the judges said anything publicly backing up his choice; not then or ever afterward.

The *Saturday Review* in 1957 published a praising review by Selden Rodman of *Hot Afternoons*. Yet it has printed nothing by Siegel in the months and years since, and refused to review his *Hail, American Development* in 1968. Rodman likewise has been silent.

A. D. Emmart of the *Baltimore Sun* knew Siegel in Baltimore when they were in school together, and was perhaps the first person to recognize his greatness. He wrote to Martha Baird in January 1969 that Siegel is the only person he ever knew of whom he would use the word "genius." Yet Emmart was literary editor of the *Baltimore Sun* in 1957 when *Hot Afternoons* appeared, and the book was not reviewed in that newspaper. Emmart has said nothing about Siegel in print, and professes—in the same 1969 letter—inability to do anything to have *Hail, American Development* reviewed.

There is much more: quoting Siegel without acknowledgment, and refusals to let statements from letters be quoted. It is a pattern in the history of Aesthetic Realism, which Martha Baird has called "The Great Enthusiasm Followed by the Great Retreat."

Dr. Williams has done better than nearly anyone in saying clearly what he saw as good. The fact that he allowed his letter to be printed shows that he did not want to repudiate it. Yet the author of *Kora in Hell* is like others in this: with gratitude and respect comes an obligation, which William Carlos Williams, at the time of his fame, saw as too large a burden.

v

It is my opinion that Eli Siegel is the greatest critic there has ever been, because he is at once the most inclusive and the most specific.

Siegel's criticism is akin to Matthew Arnold's in exactitude. Yet Matthew Arnold, whom I care for, did not see that what made for "high seriousness" was what people wanted every hour; and he did not say that the grand style had in a particular manner the great oneness of opposites which represents all reality.

Siegel has a relation to Coleridge, the first critic to state explicitly that the poetic imagination reconciles "opposite or discordant qualities."[16] Yet Coleridge did not see that opposites have to do with all the arts, and are crucial in every aspect of a poem—every time a vowel and consonant are together well—and in poems of every style. Nor did Coleridge see the conflict between thought and action, the permanent and the transitory, which tormented him in his life, as having to do with the poetic question.

Siegel is the only critic I know who can take up a poem word by word, look at every syllable, and have one feel that the universe is present as those sounds meet, and make one see technically why. And every line of good poetry, he has shown, solves the questions of our lives—because in its music, in the way syllables

16. Samuel Taylor Coleridge, Chapter XIV, *Biographia Literaria*.

are together and separate, heavy and light, it makes one opposing things, like energy and repose, order and freedom, what is hidden and what is revealed, a particular self and the world.

Eli Siegel is the critic who has shown why poetry is necessary. And the way he spoke in 1952 made Williams, troubled about the goodness of his work, feel surer that he had done something of permanent value.

And Siegel's attitude did not change with the change in Williams. There is a continuity of tone going through the 1934 *Scribner's* review (when he did not know Williams), the 1952 talk when Williams was present, and the writings of 1955 and 1967 after he had been very much hurt by Williams. There is pleasure, warmth, affection in his praise, and this is unaltered by personal circumstances. Compare, for instance, Hazlitt's veering about Coleridge and Wordsworth as his personal relations with them changed—and Hazlitt was a very fine critic. Siegel's fairness is extraordinary in criticism as it is in life. Because of it, he is able to write about himself, too, with exactitude and perspective.

Williams asked often, Why has Siegel not "pushed himself forward" and seemed incredulous that he had chosen not to. I think Siegel does want things other people want, and that he has been hurt and weakened by the lack of recognition, the injustice he has met. I am certain he has seen the fame he could have had as most attractive. But there is a need which he will not tamper with or lessen to be just to every person and object that he meets: to see all that it has in it, and its relation to the whole world. It is this need that impelled "Hot Afternoons Have Been in Montana," which Williams met with corresponding greatness. And it is the critical continuation of that impulse which affected Williams in the ways these pages document.

The history of William Carlos Williams and Eli Siegel shows that man's deepest desire, to be known, can be met.

The world is waiting to be known; Earth, what it has in it! The past is in it[17]

—Siegel wrote in 1925. In 1951, William Carlos Williams said it was necessary that the meaning of "Hot Afternoons Have Been in Montana" be welcomed by America. He is right today. Williams' judgment of Siegel, his pleasure and his gratitude, arose from the art in him—that which caused "The Red Wheelbarrow." When the art in a person speaks, the criticism that has been these centuries tells us, what we are hearing is the world.

17. "Hot Afternoons Have Been in Montana," *Hot Afternoons,* p. 6.

Appendix

1964   June 24, letter from Definition Press to New Directions stating intention to publish Siegel's March 1952
talk on Williams' poetry. Information concerning
fees for quotations of Williams' poems requested.
Also it was suggested that if New Directions, as
longtime publishers of Williams, wished to undertake the work, an arrangement could be made.

July 6, reply from James Laughlin stating fee per
line for complete poems or parts of poems where
more than ten lines is quoted. Due to overcrowded
schedule, he said, New Directions was unable to
publish the work.

The total amount of the fees made publication
impracticable for Definition Press.

Dorothy Koppelman, director of the Terrain Gallery, expressed a desire to have excerpts from the
recording of Siegel's talk with Williams' comments
played at the Terrain Gallery, and suggested a
mimeographed publication of these excerpts with
minimal quotations from Williams' poems.

October 17, 1964, the recording was played and
the mimeographed excerpts issued at the same

time with the title *Williams' Poetry Talked about by Eli Siegel, and William Carlos Williams Present and Talking: 1952*.

Subsequent interest in this publication on the part of scholars doing research on W. C. Williams stimulated a demand for it in libraries, with the result that the Terrain Gallery edition was exhausted.

1968   February 13, Definition Press again wrote to New Directions, expressing the desire to publish the entire work, with complete quotations, and again requesting permission and information as to fees.

February 23, New Directions replied that in keeping with the wishes of Mrs. Williams they were unable to grant permission.

March 8, in response to Definition Press's query, *Why?*, James Laughlin for New Directions quoted Mrs. Williams more explicitly, saying she did not wish any of William Carlos Williams' poems republished in connection with Eli Siegel's lecture.

March 19, in response to Definition Press's protest at the injustice of this, James Laughlin said the decision was final.

1969   Definition Press, having looked into the legalities of the matter, felt the right of Mrs. Williams to prevent the publication of the material on these grounds was doubtful, and wrote once more to New Directions. The letter was signed by Martha Baird, Dorothy Koppelman, Sheldon Kranz, and Ellen Reiss.

February 14, James Laughlin replied that the reason Mrs. Williams gave was that William Carlos

Williams had altered his position as to the literary theories of Eli Siegel. Mr. Laughlin's letter concluded with a paragraph on the "fair use" provision of the copyright law.

February 21, a letter from Definition Press with the same four signatures requested Mrs. Williams to read W. C. Williams' letter of 1951 again. He expressed no opinion of Eli Siegel's literary theories, but said explicitly, "It's all right to speak of aesthetic realism. . . . But it goes deeper than that —or until I understand you better I have to assume it." To this letter there was no reply.

Index

Aesthetic Method in Self-Conflict, The (ES), vii, 12, 13, 21, 110, 120

Aesthetic Realism, vi, vii, 7, 12, 13, 14, 35, 36, 57, 72, 118, 180, 181, 184, 185, 192

Al que quiere (WCW), 41

"An Old Time Raid" (WCW), 51-52

Antheil, George, 94

Anthologie de la nouvelle poésie américaine (ed. Jolas), 29

Antioch Review, 169

Arensberg, Walter Conrad, 45

Aristotle, 185

Arnold, Matthew, 112, 193

Art of William Carlos Williams, The (Guimond), 178

"Ash Wednesday" (Eliot), 65, 143-144

"Asphodel, That Greeny Flower" (WCW), 159, 161-162, 190-191

Auden, W. H., 54, 177, 188

Austen, Jane, 164

Autobiography of William Carlos Williams, The, 3, 36, 57, 69, 70, 95, 100, 166

Baird, Martha (Mrs. Eli Siegel), vi, 11, 101, 102, 113, 192, 198

Journal, 14, 16, 17-28, 30-32, 109-111, 114-115, 116-122, 122-124, 130-136

Letters, 3-4, 10, 16-17, 124-130

Baltimore Sun, 116, 134, 192

Baudelaire, 22, 69

Beaudoin, Kenneth, 27, 118

Bentham, Jeremy, 61

Berne, Stanley Lawrence, 27, 118

Bibliography of William Carlos Williams, A (Wallace), 178-179

Biographia Literaria, 146, 193

Blake, William, 154

Blues, 4

Boccaccio, 101

Bollingen jury, 134

Boone, Daniel, 165

Boyle, Kay, 176

Bready, James, 134

Brown, T. E., 88-89

Bryant, William Cullen, 160

Burr, Aaron, 59

"By the road to the contagious hospital." *See* "Spring and All"

Cairns, Huntington, 121, 134

Calisher, Hortense, 164

Carson, Rachel, 98-99

Catling, Patrick Skene, 116

Cellini, 166

Chaucer, 100, 101
Christabel, 65-66
City Lights Books, 67 n, 136
Clarke & Way, 131
Clarke, Bert, 131
Cole, William, 132
Coleridge, 65-66, 74, 146, 185, 193, 194
Collected Earlier Poems of William Carlos Williams, The, 31, 51 n
Collected Later Poems of William Carlos Williams, The, 31, 36, 79
Collected Poems (1934) (WCW), 17, 39, 54, 194
"Comedy Entombed: 1930" (WCW), 59-60
"Convivio" (WCW), 36-37
"Country Rain" (WCW), 61-62
Crashaw, Richard, 146
Cummings, E. E., 90
"Cure, The" (WCW), 92-93
"Cymon and Iphigenia" (Dryden), 100, 101

Dante, 70
"Dawn" (WCW), 159
"Dawn of Another Day" (WCW), 61
"Dear Birds, Tell This to Mothers" (ES), 135
De Baggio, Thomas, 147, 171
Definition Press, 125, 130
"Deirdre" (Stephens), 113
Derwood, Gene, 133
"Descent of Winter, The" (WCW), 17
De Soto, 165
Dial, 68
Dienes, Louis, 31, 101
"Doria" (Pound), 47
Dryden, 100, 101

Elegant Extracts (New Elegant Extracts) (ed. Hazlitt), 101
Eliot, T. S., 22, 37-38, 41-42, 43, 45, 48-49, 54, 65, 69-70, 92, 97, 141-146, 176, 187
Emerson, 50
Emmart, A. D., 192
"Eve" (WCW), 79

Farrell's Bookstore, 134
Faulk, John Henry, 132-133
"Fine Work with Pitch and Copper" (WCW), 91
Fitts, Dudley, 134
"Flower in the Crannied Wall" (Tennyson), 86
"Flower, The" (WCW), 89-90
Folio, 122-123
Four Seas Company, 42, 67
Frankenberg, Lloyd, 23, 30, 185
Free verse, 27, 46, 49, 65, 163
Frost, Robert, 176
Funk and Wagnalls' *Practical Standard Dictionary,* 45

Gannett, Lewis, 192
"Garden, The" (Brown), 88-89
Garland, Judy, 26
Gascoyne, David, 30, 31, 109, 185
Gillespie, Lincoln, 46
Ginny. *See* Williams, Mrs. Paul
Ginsberg, Allen, 175-176, 187
Golden Goose Press, 14
Goldring, Douglas, 45
Good Morning, America (Sandburg), 68

Great American Novel, The
  (WCW), 164
Greek Anthology, 67
Guimond, James, 178

Hail, American Development
  (ES), 192
Hamlet, 85, 105, 116, 168,
  188
"Hamlet Revisited" (ES),
  98, 114, 120
Harmon, Theodora, 135
Hazlitt, 101, 146, 194
Heal, Edith, 137
Hegel, 183, 185
Heraclitus, 185
Herz, Nat, 116, 122 n, 125
Herzberg, Max J., 133
*History of English Prose
  Rhythm, The* (Saintsbury),
  75
"Hollow Men, The" (Eliot),
  48-49
Hollow Reed, The (Wrinn),
  133
Holmes, Lawrence Richard,
  130 n
"Hot Afternoons Have Been
  in Montana," vii, 4, 7, 14,
  16, 24, 27, 35, 115, 118,
  122 n, 125, 175 n, 179, 187,
  192, 194-195
*Hot Afternoons Have Been
  in Montana: Poems,* 5, 130-
  136, 149, 169, 171, 192
Houghton Mifflin, 124
Hound & Horn, 4
Howl (Ginsberg), 175-176
Hoyt, Helen, 45
Hunt, Leigh, 67-68

In Defense of Ignorance
  (Shapiro), 175 n, 187 n
Indiana, University of, 122

*Influence du symbolisme
  français sur la poésie
  américaine, l'* (Taupin),
  40
"In Northern Waters"
  (WCW), 62-63
Instigations (Pound), 42-43
In the American Grain
  (WCW), 21, 49, 59, 80,
  163, 165
Ion, (Plato), 143
"It Stays Because It Is So
  Much" (ES), 113, 118
I Wanted to Write a Poem
  (WCW, ed. Heal), 137
"I—/Why?" *See* "One Ques-
  tion"

Jeffers, Robinson, 54, 176
Jerome, Judson, 169
Jolas, Eugène, 29, 30, 56
Joyce, James, 177

Kandinsky, Vasili, 73
Kant, 183
Knife of the Times, The
  (WCW), 51
Koch, Vivienne, 31, 39, 40, 63,
  64, 103, 185
Koppelman, Dorothy, 117, 197,
  198
Kora in Hell (WCW), 21,
  41, 66-67, 69, 70-83, 91,
  94, 103-105, 136-137,
  163
Korea, 96
Kranz, Sheldon, 3, 93, 103,
  117, 128, 198
Kreymborg, Alfred, 11, 46-
  47
Krutch, Joseph Wood, 191

Landor, Walter Savage, 145
Lao-tzu, 185

Laughlin, James, 147, 149, 151, 171, 197-199
Lawrence, D. H., 21-22, 165
Lectures on the English Poets (Hazlitt), 146
Lekberg, Barbara, 95, 99, 105, 128
"Let the Seeing Go On" (ES), 116 n
Library of Congress, 120, 121
Line. *See* Poetic line
Lougee, David, 27, 118
"Love Song of J. Alfred Prufrock, The" (Eliot), 48, 141-142
Lowell, Robert, 186-188
Loy, Mina, 42

McAlmon, Robert, 105, 177
McDowell, David, 188
MacLeish, Archibald, 54
Make Light of It (WCW), 51, 61, 75
Mallarmé, Stéphane, 49
"Marriage Poem" (ES), 20, 26, 110
Matthiessen, F. O., 94
"Meant To Be" (ES), 29-30, 118
Metastasio, 72
"Metric Figure" (WCW), 159
Modern Quarterly, 4
Mondlin, Marvin, 131, 132, 133, 134
Monroe, Harriet, 177
"Montana." *See* "Hot Afternoons Have Been in Montana"
Moore, Marianne, 42, 45, 147-148, 166, 179
Mother Goose, 143
Museum of Modern Art, v, 14, 23, 27, 28, 30, 110, 114, 117-119, 186, 188

"My Heart Laid Bare" (Baudelaire), 22

Nation, vi, 4, 130, 192
National Book Awards, 135-136
New Directions, 31, 147, 171
New Poems (ed. Oscar Williams), 93
New Yorker, 99
New York Times, 133, 134
"Nightingales, The" (WCW), 150, 159, 161-162
Norse, Harold, 27, 30, 31, 109, 118
"Notes on the Telephone" (ES), 134

Off to Arcady (ed. Herzberg), 133
Olney, Austin G., 124, 130
"One Question" ("I—/Why?") (ES), 5, 118, 133
Oregon Trail, The, 77
Others (ed. Kreymborg), 45-46, 50

Paradiso, 70
Parkman, Francis, 77
"Pastoral" (WCW), 52-54
Paterson, vi, 40-41, 66, 69, 72, 73, 81, 82-85, 151, 162, 187-188
Pearson, Leon, 132
Persephone, 79
Plato, 143
Poe, Edgar Allan, 49-50, 163, 165
"Poem" ("As the cat") (WCW), 89, 150-151, 166
"Poem on Lagoons" (ES), 132

Poems of William Carlos Williams, The (Wagner), 178

Poetic line, 20, 44, 77, 162, 163, 187, 189, 193-194

Poetry, 122n, 135

Poetry and Prose of Walt Whitman, The (ed. Untermeyer), 144

"Poetry and Technique" (ES), 11, 12, 13, 14, 15, 110, 184

Poetry Public, 130 n

Pope, Alexander, 145

Port of New York (Rosenfeld), 150

"Portrait of the Author" (WCW), 29, 56-57, 105, 144-145

"Postlude" (WCW), 57, 159

Pound, Ezra, 42-43, 45, 47-48, 72, 163, 176, 187

Pride and Prejudice, 164

Princeton, 21

Publishers' Weekly, 135-136

Quantum theory, 44-45, 189

"Ralph Isham, 1753 and Later" (ES), 4, 131-132

"Rapid Transit" (WCW), 90-91

"Raven, The" (Poe), 49

"Red-Haired Man's Wife, The" (Stephens), 113

"Red Lily, The" (WCW), 17-18

"Red Wheelbarrow, The" (WCW), 4, 17, 39, 85-89, 92, 143-144, 155-159

Reiss, Ellen, 198

Rexroth, Kenneth, 133

Rimbaud, 69, 74

Robbins, Louis, 128, 132

Robbins, Mrs. Louis, 128

Robinson, Edwin Arlington, 54, 92, 176

"Rock, The" (Eliot), 145-146

Rodman, Selden, 133, 134-135, 192

Rosenfeld, Paul, 11, 149-150, 166

Rosenthal, M. L., 147-161 *passim*, 167

Rousseau, 166

St. Louis Blues, 55

Saintsbury, George, 68, 75, 112

Sanborn, Pitts, 45

Sandburg, Carl, 45, 68, 177

Saturday Review, 133, 134-135, 192

Scribner's 11, 37, 38, 194

Sea Around Us, The (Carson), 98-99

"Sea-Elephant, The" (WCW), 49

Selected Letters of William Carlos Williams, The (ed. Thirlwall), 136, 149, 178, 179, 186, 187, 188

Seventeenth-Century Lyrics (ed. Saintsbury), 68

Shakespeare, 100, 101-103

Shapiro, Karl, 122 n, 175, 187 n

Shelley, 26

"She's Crazy and It Means Something" (ES), 5, 118, 135

"Shop Girl" (Pound), 47-48

"Shortest Poem in the World, The." *See* "One Question"

Siegel, Eli
  Letters, 11-14, 15-16, 16-17, 28-30, 111-114, 115, 122

Siegel, Eli (*continued*)
  Review of Williams' *Collected Poems* (1934), 38-39, 194
  Telephone conversation with WCW, 120-121
  Aesthetic Method in Self-Conflict, vii, 12, 13, 21, 110, 120
  "Dear Birds, Tell This to Mothers," 135
  Hail, American Development, 192
  "Hamlet Revisited," 98, 114, 120
  "Hot Afternoons Have Been in Montana," vii, 4, 7, 14, 16, 24, 27, 35, 115, 118, 122 n, 125, 175 n, 179, 187, 192, 194-195
  Hot Afternoons Have Been in Montana: Poems, 5, 130-136, 149, 169, 171, 192
  "It Stays Because It Is So Much," 113, 118
  "I—/Why?" *See* "One Question"
  "Let the Seeing Go On," 116 n
  "Marriage Poem," 20, 26, 110
  "Meant To Be," 29-30, 118
  "Notes on the Telephone," 134
  "One Question" ("I—/Why?"), 5, 118, 133
  "Poem on Lagoons," 132
  "Poetry and Technique," 11, 12, 13, 14, 15, 110, 184
  "Ralph Isham, 1753 and Later," 4, 131-132
  "She's Crazy and It Means Something," 5, 118, 135

"World of the Unwashed Dish," 135
"Worms Go South and They Fit In," 4, 132
Siegel, Mrs. Eli. *See* Baird, Martha
Silver Treasury of Light Verse, The (ed. Oscar Williams), 133
Singer, Barbara, 109
Sitwell, Edith, 177
Society for Aesthetic Realism, 3, 4, 12, 31
Sonnet, 46, 99-100
Sonnet 107 (Shakespeare), 101-102
Sonnets (Shakespeare), 102, 103
Sour Grapes (WCW), 41, 56
Spender, Stephen, 54
Spring and All (WCW), 41
"Spring and All" (WCW), 64-65
Starrels, Nancy, 103, 123-124, 128, 130
Stendhal, 60
Stephens, James, 113
Stevens, Wallace, 45, 176, 185
"Sun Bathers, The" (WCW), 91

Taupin, René, 39-40
Tempers, The (WCW), 41
Tennyson, 86, 88
"Term, The" (WCW), 81
Terrain Gallery, v, 197
"There Was a Child Went Forth" (Whitman), 80
Thirlwall, John C., 123, 130, 136, 149, 170, 178, 186, 188-190
Thompson, Francis, 146
"To One in Paradise" (Poe), 49-50
Toynbee, Arnold, 8

"Tract" (WCW), 50-51, 53
Transition, 94
Tristram (Robinson), 92
"Two Pendants" (WCW), 79

Underground, 147
Untermeyer, Louis, 23, 31, 118, 133, 144, 185

Van Doren, Mark, 31, 191
"Verbal Transcription— 6 A.M." (WCW), 63-64
Villon, 49
"Vista" (Kreymborg), 46-47
Voyage to Pagany, A (WCW), 57-58, 59, 86, 90, 94-95, 164

Wagner, Linda, 178
Wallace, Emily Mitchell, 178-179
Washington, George, 59
Washington Independent, 147, 149, 171
Waste Land, The (Eliot), 37, 41-42, 48
Way, David J., 131, 133
Weaver, Michael, 170-171
Webster, Daniel, 26
Welty, Eudora, 164
Wheeler, Monroe, 117
Whitman, 80, 144, 146, 189
"Widow's Lament in Spring-time, The" (WCW), 164
William Carlos Williams Reader, The (ed. Rosenthal), 147-167, 171
Williams, Mrs. Paul (Virginia) (Ginny), 19, 22, 24, 30, 31, 119-120, 122
Williams, Mrs. William Carlos (Florence), v, 11, 15, 16, 19, 24-25, 119, 185, 190, 198, 199
Williams, Oscar, 93, 133

Williams, Paul, 19
Williams' Poetry Talked about by Eli Siegel, and William Carlos Williams Present and Talking: 1952, 171, 198
Williams, William Carlos
  1951 Letter to Martha Baird, v, vi, 6-10, 12, 20, 96, 122-130 *passim*, 148, 149, 169, 170, 171, 175 n, 177-178, 183-184, 189, 190, 199
  Al que quiere, 41
  "An Old Time Raid," 51-52
  "Asphodel, That Greeny Flower," 159, 161-162, 190-191
  Autobiography, 3, 36, 57, 69, 70, 95, 100, 166
  "By the road to the contagious hospital." *See* "Spring and All"
  Collected Earlier Poems, 31
  Collected Later Poems, 31, 36, 79
  Collected Poems (1934), 17, 39, 54, 194
  "Comedy Entombed: 1930," 59-60
  "Convivio," 36-37
  "Country Rain," 61-62
  "Cure," 92-93
  "Dawn," 159
  "Dawn of Another Day," 61
  "Descent of Winter," 17
  "Eve," 79
  "Fine Work with Pitch and Copper," 91
  "Flower," 89-90
  Great American Novel, 164
  "In Northern Waters," 62-63
  In the American Grain, 21, 49, 59, 80, 163, 165
  I Wanted to Write a Poem, 137

Williams, W. C. (*continued*)
  Knife of the Times, 51
  Kora in Hell, 21, 41, 66-67,
    69, 70-83, 91, 94, 103-
    105, 136-137, 163
  Make Light of It, 51, 61, 75
  "Metric Figure," 159
  "Nightingales," 150, 159,
    161-162
  "Pastoral," 52-54
  Paterson, vi, 40-41, 66, 69,
    72, 73, 81, 82-85, 151,
    162, 187-188
  "Poem." ("As the cat"),
    89, 150-151, 166
  "Portrait of the Author,"
    29, 56-57, 105, 144-145
  "Postlude," 57, 159
  "Rapid Transit," 90-91
  "Red Lily," 17-18
  "Red Wheelbarrow," 4, 17,
    39, 85-89, 92, 143-144,
    155-159
  "Sea-Elephant," 49
  Selected Letters, 136, 149,
    178, 179, 186, 187, 188
  Sour Grapes, 41, 56
  Spring and All, 41
  "Spring and All," 64-65
  "Sun Bathers," 91
  Tempers, 41

  "Term," 81
  "Tract," 50-51, 53
  "Two Pendants," 79
  "Verbal Transcription—
    6 A.M." 63-64
  Voyage to Pagany, 57-58,
    59, 86, 90, 94-95, 164
  "Widow's Lament in
    Springtime," 164
  *William Carlos Williams
    Reader,* 147-167, 171
  "Yachts," 93-94, 145, 159,
    161-162
  "Young Sycamore," 54-55,
    142-143
Wordsworth, 100, 194
"World of the Unwashed Dish,
  The" (ES) 135
"Worms Go South and They
  Fit In" (ES), 4, 132
Wrinn, Mary J. J., 133

"Yachts, The" (WCW), 93-94,
  145, 159, 161-162
Yeats, William Butler, 66
"Young Sycamore" (WCW),
  54-55, 142-143

Zillman, Lawrence John, 133
Zorach, William, 46